Brokenness

THE
HEART
GOD
REVIVES

Revive Our Hearts
SERIES

Brokenness

THE
HEART
GOD
REVIVES

NANCY LEIGH DeMOSS

MOODY PRESS
CHICAGO

All Scripture quotations, unless otherwise indicated, are taken from the *New King James Version*. Copyright © 1982 by Thomas Nelson, Inc. Used by permission. All rights reserved.

Scripture quotations marked KJV are taken from the King James Version.

ISBN: 0-8024-1275-0

1 3 5 7 9 10 8 6 4 2

Printed in the United States of America

L ord, High and Holy, meek and lowly,
Thou hast brought me to the valley of vision,
  where I live in the depths but see thee in the heights;
  hemmed in by mountains of sin I behold thy glory.

Let me learn by paradox
  that the way down is the way up,
  that to be low is to be high,
  that the broken heart is the healed heart,
  that the contrite spirit is the rejoicing spirit,
  that the repenting soul is the victorious soul,
  that to have nothing is to possess all,
  that to bear the cross is to wear the crown,
  that to give is to receive,
  that the valley is the place of vision.
Lord, in the daytime stars can be seen from deepest wells,
  and the deeper the wells the brighter thy stars shine;
Let me find thy light in my darkness,
        thy life in my death,
        thy joy in my sorrow,
        thy grace in my sin,
        thy riches in my poverty,
        thy glory in my valley.

—from *The Valley of Vision: A Collection of
Puritan Prayers and Devotions*

CONTENTS

FOREWORD

In November 2001, I witnessed an incredible moving of God upon more than 500 pastors and other leaders in Korea. God's presence came suddenly, and with profound and thorough conviction of sin, bringing deep repentance and personal and corporate brokenness. Some were before the Lord all night before He would let them go. They were convinced that God was inviting them to see their sin as He saw it, to quickly and thoroughly forsake their sins, and to be ready as clean vessels of the Lord to guide His people in a fresh time of revival in their land (Acts 3:19).

It was an awesome sight and sound to hear and see the wailing before the Lord in genuine repentance, cleansing, and brokenness and to hear the expectant cries for revival among God's people and for spiritual awakening in their nation. They were especially grieved over the lost condition of their countrymen in North Korea.

Utter brokenness in God's holy presence is a prerequisite to any mighty moving of God in revival. I was with Nancy Leigh DeMoss in Fort Collins, Colorado, in July 1995, when utter brokenness occurred, an event she so adequately relates in this book. Nancy describes her own response to God's touch on His people and on our lives also. Truly, neither of us will ever be the same again.

May this be repeated all across our nation as we take seriously what God is saying to His pastors, leaders, and people. It remains absolutely true today that:

IF God permits crises, as spoken by God:

When I shut up heaven and there is no rain, or command the locusts to devour the land, or send pestilence among My people . . . (2 Chronicles 7:13)

THEN

if My people who are called by My name will humble themselves, and pray and seek My face, and turn from their wicked ways, then I will hear from heaven, and will forgive their sin and heal their land (2 Chronicles 7:14).

I believe God is saying one more time:

Now My eyes will be open and My ears attentive . . . (2 Chronicles 7:15).

I am making clear and strong changes in my life for these days, praying that a much-needed revival may come to our nation and our world. I am especially seeking opportunities for personal revival and prayer.

I want to challenge you to heed the call that God has so clearly given to Nancy: a call to brokenness. Give careful attention to her helpful guidance in practically implementing this message in your life, your family, and your church. Make the adjustments in your life to God immediately and thoroughly.

Much of our world is making major adjustments to the new realities we now face as a result of September 11, 2001. Will God's leaders and God's people continue with *business as usual?* We must not! Since many do not know how to identify spiritual crises, and therefore do not know clearly what to do before God, this book will be both a very timely word from God and a practical guide to returning to God, so He can work once again through His people toward revival and spiritual awakening.

—Henry T. Blackaby

ACKNOWLEDGMENTS

More than any other message I have written or shared from the platform, the "credit" for this particular message should rightly be shared with others. Many of the components of this book—including specific scriptural insights, applications, and, in a few cases, actual wording —were developed over several years in collaboration with the staff of Life Action Ministries, particularly *Del Fehsenfeld Jr.* (now with the Lord) and *Tim St. Clair,* as we served together in revival ministry.

Over the years, Tim, Del, and I have exchanged insights and notes and delivered similar messages, making it difficult to know with certainty at points "who first said what." The heart of these men is such that they have never sought credit for their work, desiring only that the message be proclaimed and heeded by the people of God. Even more than the content of their messages, their lives have shown me the meaning of true brokenness. This book is the fruit of our combined labors and partnership in ministry.

Others have also made a significant contribution to this work. Special appreciation is due to:

Lela Gilbert and *Cheryl Dunlop* for their editorial efforts that have helped me to communicate my heart more effectively.

Greg Thornton, Bill Thrasher, Elsa Mazon, and my other friends at Moody Press, without whose vision, support, and partnership this book would not have been birthed.

The men and women who serve on the staff of Revive Our Hearts, and whose faithful, diligent efforts make it possible for me to focus on developing and presenting the message of revival.

Acknowledgments

My team of Praying Friends, whose intercession before the Throne has been the means of great grace in my life, and whose encouragement has often helped me press on when I felt I had nothing left to give.

Far surpassing all other contributors is *my precious Lord Jesus,* whose brokenness continues to call me to brokenness, and whose sacrifice at Calvary makes the offering of my heart and of this book acceptable to the Father.

INTRODUCTION

Come as the fire, and purge our hearts
With sacrificial flame;
Let our whole soul an offering be
To our Redeemer's Name.

—ANDREW REED

In July 1995, anticipation was unusually high as four thousand staff members of Campus Crusade for Christ converged on Moby Gym at Colorado State University in Ft. Collins, Colorado, from all across the United States. Throughout the preceding spring, spiritual stirrings had been spontaneously ignited at a number of college campuses—some Christian, some secular. A number of Campus Crusade staff members had witnessed these events firsthand and were eager to see God do more.

Desiring a fresh work of God among their staff, the ministry leadership had been prompted to make revival the focus of their biannual staff conference. The seriousness of their intent was seen when they agreed to depart from their normal schedule and to set apart extended times each morning during the weeklong conference for the staff to seek the Lord. Only one or two speakers were scheduled for each of these extended sessions. No time limitations were placed on the speakers. Significant blocks of time were simply left open to see how God would lead.

The conference began on Friday with a day of worship, prayer, and fasting. The corporate sense of longing for God to move was palpable at points. The prayers and longing intensified over the next few days as the staff heard messages from men such as Dr. Bill Bright about "first love" for Jesus, and Dennis Rainey about the need to honor parents. There were also a number of firsthand reports from some who had witnessed what God had done on college campuses that spring.

Several months earlier, knowing of my burden for revival, the leadership had asked if I would address the staff at this particular gathering. Feeling keenly the responsibility of this assignment, I had been waiting on the Lord for direction for my message. Not until two weeks before the conference did I finally sense what I was to address—the subject of brokenness and humility. The burden emerged out of study and meditation I had been doing in the book of Isaiah for several months. It also came out of a work that God had been doing in my own heart. He had recently brought me to a new level of repentance and brokenness in a particular issue in my life.

> GOD WANTS TO REVEAL HIS PRESENCE AND GLORY TO HIS PEOPLE.

On Monday morning, I stood to speak to a group of Christian workers whom God had been preparing for this moment. I spoke with the staff about what God had been teaching me about the meaning of true brokenness. About ten minutes before the end of the message, out of the corner of my eye I noticed two men who had slipped out of their seats somewhere in that vast room and had walked to the front of the gym. They quietly knelt on the floor in front of the platform where I was speaking. To this day, I have no idea who those men were or exactly why they came. But in retrospect, I believe their humility set the stage and paved the way for the brokenness and humility of others.

At the close of the message, I referred to an old Gospel song that had been sung in many of the student revivals of the past spring:

> Pass me not, O gentle Savior,
> Hear my humble cry;
> While on others Thou art calling,
> Do not pass me by.

I suggested that we sing that song and encouraged those present to take any step of humility and brokenness that God was putting on their hearts. As I recall, that was at about 10:30 in the morning. What happened over the next hours and days is almost too sacred and precious to describe. In fact, this is the first time I have attempted to write about that week—I did not even record it in my personal journal.

I have struggled with whether or not I should write even this brief account. I tremble at the thought that I might in any way deflect any credit or glory for that divine visitation away from God. I know all too well that I had nothing to do with what took place—that I was (and am) more a candidate for revival than in any way responsible for it. I know, and will tell in the pages that follow, some of the battles of my own heart with the deadly sin of pride—the very thing I felt led to address and expose that day.

What has compelled me to proceed is the conviction that what God did in Moby Gym that week was just a glimpse of what He longs to do throughout Christendom. He wants to reveal His presence and glory to His people. He wants to fill our hearts and homes, our churches and ministries with His love and His Spirit. He wants to pour out His grace on the dry, thirsty ground of our lives.

He wants to restore our "first love" for Jesus, rekindle the fire of devotion that once burned brightly in our hearts, reconcile broken relationships, and rebuild the parts of our lives that are in a state of disrepair. In short, He wants to revive our hearts. *And it all begins with brokenness and humility.* No exceptions. No shortcuts. No substitutes.

No human fully knows or could possibly capture what took place that hot July day in Colorado. But I believe most who were present would agree that God was there and that His presence was manifest in an extraordinary way. As He began to move in the hearts of His people, all scheduled events for the rest of the day were canceled; the same thing happened the next day and half of the following day. There were no official breaks during the service that began at 9:00 Monday morning and continued until midnight that night. Most of those in attendance had no desire to leave, though some slipped in and out as necessary for physical nourishment or to tend to needs of children. Throughout the day, hour after hour,

> PRETENSE AND MASKS WERE STRIPPED OFF IN HIS PRESENCE.

people stayed glued to their seats on the main floor or in the bleachers as we waited, listened, repented, prayed, and worshiped.

Moby Gym is just that—a gym—home of the Colorado State Rams. It is not the kind of setting where one would ordinarily expect to encounter God. But that week it became a sanctuary—a holy place where the presence of God was experienced in an unusual way among His people. The entire room became an altar where men and women made a living sacrifice of their lives to the Lord. Throughout that vast auditorium, hundreds of men and women humbled themselves before God and before one another. Husbands and wives, parents and young people, colleagues, supervisors and subordinates—people got serious about being honest with God and with each other. Over the next few days, long-standing grievances were confessed and breaches were reconciled—some of them going back for decades.

Under the Spirit's conviction, scores and scores of men and women came to the microphone to confess specific sins before God and their fellow workers. Pretense and masks were stripped off in His presence. Spiritual needs and failures were confessed openly. At midnight on Monday night, when the decision was made to break for sleep and resume the next day, staff members were still standing in line waiting to reach the microphone.

One of the most vivid memories I have of that week is a scene that took place again and again: As each person finished his or her confession, ten, twenty, thirty, or even fifty or more people would leave their seats, rushing to encircle the person and pray for him or her. At any given time there were several of these groups praying near the platform. Earnest intercession poured forth on behalf of broken believers who were repenting of every conceivable sin and bondage.

The brokenness that flowed in that room was both intensely personal and profoundly corporate. What a fragrance must have wafted up to the throne of God as this family of believers repented and humbled themselves before Him.

Not everything that took place during those days was neat, clean, and easy to explain. Revival can be messy. It was as if a large rock had been overturned and a floodlight turned on, exposing all kinds of worms and insects. Not everyone was comfortable with the public nature of the confessions. But there was a widespread sense that what was happening was not man-initiated, and that trying to control it would have been like standing in front of a fast-moving freight train and telling it to stop.

The leaders of the ministry were united in their concern not to quench or grieve the Holy Spirit in any way. From hour to hour, they sought the Lord as to "what next?" Should they let this continue? (To do so meant dispensing with other scheduled speakers and training sessions.) How and to what extent should it be steered? (In a group that size there were also practical considerations—what about the fifteen hundred children in child care?) In the midst of a stirring of God's Spirit, there are no "experts." Nothing anyone had read or experienced had prepared them to know how to "manage" this moment. That, too, was humbling.

DO YOU NEED A FRESH INFUSION OF THE GRACE OF GOD IN YOUR LIFE?

In God's providence, Dr. Henry Blackaby, author of *Experiencing God,* had been invited to speak to the staff. When he arrived that first evening, he sat and listened and prayed as person after person unburdened his heart and expressed his need for a fresh cleansing and filling of the Spirit. The next morning, he preached an anointed message on the nature of true repentance. Then for the next seven or eight hours, he stood by the side of others who came to the microphone to confess the issues over which God had convicted their hearts. His pastoral, biblical input helped people move into thorough, genuine repentance.

The truth that God used to bring His children into a new level of freedom and fruitfulness that week is intended to be a way of life for every believer. Yet, by and large, it is a missing element in evangelicalism today. With all our talk of worship, unity, reconciliation, love, and the power of God, we have bypassed the essential ingredient that makes these things possible. I believe a return to this truth—the need for brokenness and humility—is the starting place for experiencing the revival we so desperately need in our lives, our homes, and our churches.

This is not a new truth. As you will see, it is a timeless principle that runs as a thread through all the Word of God. It is the only way you and I can draw near to a holy God. It is God's prescription for nearly every condition that ails human hearts and relationships. Loneliness, fear, sinful bondages, fragmented relationships, communication barriers, generation gaps, unresolved conflicts, guilt, shame, self-absorption, addictions, hypocrisy, and at times even shyness—all these issues and more have their root in pride; but they can crumble through genuine brokenness and humility.

Do you need a fresh infusion of the grace of God in your life? Do you long to experience the abundant life, to live in the realm of the supernatural, and to enjoy the free flow of God's Spirit in your life? Do you want to be set free from those selfish, sinful patterns that plague your walk and poison your relationships? Do you want to find fullness of joy? Does your heart need to be revived?

This book is an invitation to encounter God in a whole new way. It is a call to discover His heart and His ways; a challenge to embrace a radically new way of thinking and living, in which the way up is down, death brings life, and brokenness is the pathway to wholeness.

1

THE HEART
of the
MATTER

It is a wonder what God can do with a broken heart,
if He gets all the pieces.
—◦ SAMUEL CHADWICK

If you were to meet Wayne and Gwyn Stanford today, you would find a tenderhearted, warm, compassionate, humble couple. If you conversed with them for any length of time, they would undoubtedly tell you something fresh that God was teaching them or doing in their lives.

It wasn't always that way. When I first met this couple more than twenty years ago, they were in their early fifties. By the world's standards, they had it made. Wayne was a successful businessman; he and Gwyn had a lovely home in the Midwest and a vacation home in Florida. They were respected leaders in their community and were active in their local church and their denomination. But, as they later said publicly, they were both afflicted with a deadly heart condition that they didn't realize they had—a malady known as *pride*.

Today they are able to see what they were blind to at the time. Gwyn admits,

> I was proud of my reputation and my position. I was known at the country club where I was an officer, known among the elite of the community, and known as a leader at my church. I was at the church every time the doors were open. It was important to me to have everyone notice me and what I was doing. I was extremely self-righteous and thought I was more spiritual than others. Others had needs, but not Gwyn Stanford. Others needed revival, but not I!

Though they both appeared to be spiritually prosperous, the truth was that their hearts were hollow, hard, and spiritually starved. "Right in the middle of religion, I was so very far away from God," Gwyn says with regret.

Though Wayne was oblivious to his own spiritual need, it was readily apparent to those around him. His pastor at the time remembers the Wayne Stanford of those days as "a cold, calculating, highly opinionated man. He almost demanded that I follow his ideas for leading the church. He was extremely judgmental and critical. Our attempted fellowships together generally ended in frustrated anger. There was a deep chasm between us."

Gwyn's heart condition manifested itself in more subtle ways:

> I was unteachable; although I was a leader, I wasn't in the Word; I lived, acted, and operated based on the world's way of thinking. I didn't know what it meant to be honest, open, and transparent before God and others. The one thing I did know was how to play church—I knew how to pretend.

Wayne and Gwyn might well have lived the rest of their lives in that condition—spiritually deceived, hardened, and unusable—had not the Lord graciously intervened to show them their need and rescue them from their pride.

In 1982 I was part of a team that was invited to minister in Wayne and Gwyn's church for a concentrated two-week period of seeking the Lord.[1] During that time, church members were challenged to face the reality of their spiritual condition. The Stanfords' lives would never be the same again as a result of that honest look.

The second Sunday morning of that series of meetings is indelibly etched on Wayne's mind. The message was based on the Old Testament story of Naaman (2 Kings 5). As the respected, capable commander in chief of the Syrian army, Naaman appeared to have it all together—except for the fact that he had leprosy. Naaman wanted to be healed, but not at the expense of his pride. Wayne was stopped short as he saw himself in this proud general:

He did what I probably would have done: he loaded up six thousand shekels of gold and ten talents of silver, and he went down to buy his way out of his problem. Right in the middle of

that message, God said to me, *You're just like
Naaman! You've got spiritual leprosy and you need
to be healed. You can be restored, but you're going to
have to do it My way.*

That morning, in the middle of the service,
Wayne made his way to a room that had been
designated for those who needed prayer—that
in itself was a big step of humility, as he had
previously determined he would not go to that
room. As he arrived at the prayer room, this respected leader fell on his knees and cried out to
God to have mercy on him; he confessed his sin
of pride and pretense, and surrendered himself
to do whatever God wanted him to do.

That same week, Gwyn attended a special
prayer meeting for the women of the church. It
was there that she had a life-changing encounter
with God. That morning the leader spoke three
words that penetrated her heart: "God is alive!"
That simple phrase wakened her from her spiritual sleep and transformed her life. She remembers thinking, *Gwyn, you're living as if God
is dead.* For the first time, she saw herself as God
saw her—and it wasn't the Gwyn who had it all

put together. She saw herself as sinful and desperately needy of His grace.

The conviction of God's Spirit was intense. For the first time in her life, she responded to that conviction in humility. In fact, she realized that, in spite of her religious appearance and activity, she had never been truly born again. She cried out to God to save her and received assurance that He had given her a new, clean heart.

ISSUES OF THE HEART

What took place in Wayne and Gwyn's lives more than two decades ago was nothing short of major heart surgery. In Gwyn's case, she had been deceived for years into believing that she was a child of God, simply because she was a faithful, active church member. She needed— and received—a heart transplant. In Wayne's case, his spiritual arteries had become hardened —clogged and crusted over with self, pride, religious works, and "keeping up appearances."

The Old Testament prophet Jeremiah understood that the heart was what mattered to God, and that if the heart were sick, the whole body would be in trouble. Relentlessly, persistently, he addressed the matter of the heart. There are more than seventy references to the heart in his writings. God gave him discernment to see beyond the impressive, external religious life of His people. Jeremiah penetrated and probed and held the people's hearts up to the light; he pleaded with them to see what God saw.

From all appearances, the Jews—God's chosen people—were deeply religious; but Jeremiah proclaimed that their hearts had turned away from the God who had redeemed them: "This people has a defiant and rebellious *heart*" (5:23, italics added, and so with all references in this chapter).

The Old Testament Jews dutifully performed countless rituals of ceremonial cleansing. But Jeremiah understood that all those physical washings were merely intended to be a picture of purity of heart, so he urged: "O Jerusalem, wash your *heart* from wickedness" (4:14).

Though God had revealed Himself and His law to the His people, their hearts were stubborn and they had become desensitized to His Word: "Each one follows the dictates [walks

after the stubbornness; marginal reading NKJV]
of his own evil *heart,* so that no one listens to
Me" (16:12).

When we open the New Testament, we encounter the Lord Jesus, God's
final Prophet, picking up the
same theme that reverberates
throughout the pages of the
Old Testament. During His
earthly ministry, He upset the
whole religious system of His
day because He refused to be

IF THEIR *HEARTS*
WEREN'T RIGHT,
THEY WEREN'T
RIGHT.

impressed with the things that men esteem
most highly and insisted on exposing the hearts
of people as what really mattered.

He looked the most religious men of His day
in the face and confronted them with the fact
that they were obsessed with putting on a good
appearance and a good performance, while
their hearts were empty and corrupt:

*Hypocrites! Well did Isaiah prophesy about you,
saying:*
   *"These people draw near to Me with their mouth,
   And honor Me with their lips,*

But their heart *is far from Me.
And in vain they worship Me."*
— Matthew 15:7–9

When the disciples asked Jesus to explain why He had been so hard on the Pharisees, He pointed out that they were fastidious about washing their hands before eating, so as not to become ceremonially defiled, but were oblivious to the corruption of their hearts: "Out of the *heart* proceed evil thoughts, murders, adulteries, fornications, thefts, false witness, blasphemies. These are the things which defile a man, but to eat with unwashed hands does not defile a man" (Matthew 15:19–20).

Over and over again, He kept coming back to the issue of the *heart*. It didn't matter if they circumcised their bodies and tithed everything they owned, down to their herbs; it didn't matter if they washed their hands every time they ate and could quote the Law from beginning to end; it didn't matter if they scrupulously observed every feast day, every fast day, and every Sabbath day; it didn't matter if everyone else respected them as devout believers—if their *hearts* weren't right, *they* weren't right.

The medical profession stresses the importance of regular physical checkups. Anyone with a family history of heart disease is encouraged to get his cholesterol tested. We don't assume that because we look fine outwardly, we have nothing to worry about. If our heart is not functioning properly or there is blockage in our arteries, we want to know about the problem so we can do whatever is necessary to deal with the situation. We know that neglecting our physical heart condition could be fatal.

Should we be any less concerned about our spiritual heart condition? The fact is, when it comes to spiritual matters, we all have a family history of "heart disease." We must be willing to let Him examine our hearts and diagnose that which we may be unable to see for ourselves.

The Good News of the Gospel is that the Great Physician has made available a cure for our deceived, diseased hearts. Jesus came to do radical heart surgery—to cleanse and transform us from the inside out, by the power of His death and resurrection. "I will cleanse you from all your filthiness and from all your idols. I will give you a new *heart* and put a new spirit within you; I will take the *heart* of stone out of your flesh and give you a *heart* of flesh. I will put My Spirit within you" (Ezekiel 36:25–27).

A COMPLETE TAKEOVER

The transformation that took place in Wayne and Gwyn Stanford's lives when God gave them new, clean hearts was dramatic. As another friend said after having a similar encounter with God, "Revival is not just an emotional touch; it's a complete takeover!"

Gwyn remembers some of the first evidences that her heart had been changed: "Immediately I became so hungry for His Word that I could hardly wait to get up in the morning to see what He was going to reveal to me. I wanted to spend time with Him. I found myself loving people I'd never loved before."

In Wayne's case, when God changed his heart, his whole demeanor changed. The same pastor who had felt the brunt of Wayne's controlling, critical spirit later wrote: "It is difficult to believe that the Wayne Stanford I first met is the same Spirit-filled, gentle, longsuffering, compassionate, prayer warrior we know today."

God began to deal with Wayne about his business and financial affairs, resulting in a radical change of values. He began to lead his family spiritually—by his example and by his words. As they began to see the reality of Christ in their parents, Wayne and Gwyn's three grown daughters —already professing believers—all came to genuine faith in Christ.

Rather than living for themselves and accumulating things for their own pleasure, Wayne and Gwyn began to look for ways to invest their time and resources to further the kingdom of Christ. A self-centered lifestyle was replaced with a sacrificial lifestyle.

The personal revival Wayne and Gwyn experienced in 1982 was not short-lived. For more than twenty years, they have continued to walk humbly with God and to love and serve Him and others. That initial "breaking point" has become an ongoing process of daily brokenness. Gwyn acknowledges that there have been ups and downs in that process:

I'm not going to tell you that I have it all together. I will tell you that I have needs and struggles. But I'm learning to acknowledge my need to God and others, and to be open, honest, and transparent. My attitude used to be, "I don't need you, but you very much need me." I was willing to help, but I was not willing to unmask and be helped. Now I know that when I humble and unmask myself, then, and only then, can I truly experience God's grace and be victorious and free.

Wayne and Gwyn discovered a secret that delivered them from religion and released them to enjoy the fullness of life in the Spirit—they learned what kind of heart God revives. They learned that God's values are not the same as man's values. They learned that real life, freedom, and joy are not to be found in climbing up the socioeconomic ladder, but in humbling ourselves; not in being self-sufficient, but in acknowledging need. They were willing to take off their religious masks and get real. And when they did, God met them in a way they had never experienced before.

HEART CHECK

What about you? What is the condition of your heart? Could it be that you, like Wayne and Gwyn, have been going through the motions, playing church, pretending that all is well, when the truth is that you need major heart surgery—perhaps even a heart transplant?

Would you be willing to make an appointment with the Great Physician, place yourself on His table, and ask Him to examine your heart? If so, pray the prayer of the psalmist: "Search me, O God, and know my heart" (Psalm 139:23).

He wants to revive our hearts. However, there is a condition that must be met if our hearts are to be revived. The truth you will read on the following pages may turn your world and your thinking upside down, as it did to those who heard it in the Bible days. At first, God's way may seem negative, confining, or painful. But, as my friends Wayne and Gwyn discovered, it is actually the pathway to freedom, fullness, victory, fruitfulness, and joy.

NOTE

1. Since 1971 teams from Life Action Ministries have conducted more than a thousand extended revival meetings in local churches. For more information about this ministry or to inquire about scheduling a team in your church, contact Life Action Ministries, P.O. Box 31, Buchanan, MI 49107; 269/684-5905; e-mail: info@LifeAction.org; www.LifeAction.org.

2

WHAT
Is
BROKENNESS?

To be broken is the beginning of revival.
It is painful, it is humiliating,
but it is the only way.

—ROY HESSION[1]

Walk through any Christian bookstore today, and you'll find an array of books and products offering to help you be successful in every dimension and season of life:

- how to find peace, happiness, and fulfillment
- how to have a more intimate marriage
- how to have a better relationship with your kids
- how to feel closer to God

- how to deal with hurts and wounds in your past
- how to get along better with people
- how to succeed at work, at school, and at home
- how to have an effective ministry
- how to grow a great church
- how to get more out of the Bible

We have more tools and resources for our questions and hurts and needs today than any time in the history of the church. Why, then, do so many Christians live frustrated, defeated, empty, barren lives? Deep down, many of us long to experience a greater reality of God's presence and power in our lives. Our hearts need to be revived. But so few voices today are pointing us to the truth that will revive our hearts and set us free.

The Scripture is clear about the kind of heart God revives. The secret that transformed Wayne and Gwyn's lives is really no secret at all. It is interwoven as a thread all through the Word of God.

For thus says the High and Lofty One
Who inhabits eternity,
whose name is Holy:
"I dwell in the high and holy place,
With him who has a contrite and humble spirit,
To revive the spirit of the humble,
And to revive the heart of the contrite ones.

— Isaiah 57:15, emphasis added,
and so through this chapter

According to this passage, God has two "addresses." The first one comes as no surprise. We are told that the high and exalted God of the universe lives in "eternity, in the high and holy place." Yet, the Scripture says, God has another "address," and I find this one astounding. He lives with those who have a humble and contrite spirit. Generally, we would think of kings as being comfortable with the high and mighty, with the wealthy and the successful. But this King chooses to dwell with those who are contrite and humble.

To what kind of person does God draw near? What kind of person does He rescue and deliver?

He is attracted to those who have a broken, contrite spirit.

Psalm 51 is the heartfelt, penitent prayer written by King David after he committed his great sin with Bathsheba. He realized that there was absolutely nothing he could do to earn his way back into God's favor. "For You do not desire sacrifice, or else I would give it; You do not delight in burnt offering" (verse 16).

David is saying, "Lord, if you wanted ten thousand sheep or oxen or bullocks, I would offer them as a sacrifice." Have you ever noticed how many people feel they need to jump through some sort of spiritual hoops to earn God's favor? David understood that God wasn't looking for religious acts or devout behavior. The only offering God really wanted was a humble, contrite heart.

> *The sacrifices of God are a*
> broken spirit,
> A broken and a contrite heart—
> *These, O God, You will not despise.*
> —Psalm 51:17

Jesus began the first recorded sermon of His earthly ministry on this same theme: "Blessed are the *poor in spirit . . .*" (Matthew 5:3). Jesus was talking about how to experience true joy—how to be happy. It begins, He explained, by being *poor.* Now in today's world, if we were asked to suggest ways to be blessed, I'm not sure we would have started in

WE WANT THE
RESURRECTION
WITHOUT GO-
ING THROUGH
THE GRAVE.

that particular place. We don't generally think of poverty as a blessing. But Jesus came to introduce a whole new economy—a radically different way of thinking about life.

In the Greek language in which the New Testament was originally written, there are two words Jesus could have chosen to speak of someone being "poor." The first word suggests someone who lives just below the poverty line, someone who is always having to scrimp and scrape to survive, someone who makes it, but barely. That is not the word Jesus chose. He used another word that means *a beggar*—a person who is utterly, absolutely destitute. This beggar has no hope of surviving unless some-body reaches out a hand and pulls him up.

What is Jesus saying? Blessed are *the beggars* —those who recognize that they are spiritually destitute and bankrupt. They know that they have no chance of survival apart from God's in-tervening mercy and grace. Because of their need, they reach out to Him. Because they reach out to Him, He responds by lavishing them with the riches of His kingdom and reviving their hearts.

Our culture is obsessed with being whole and feeling good. That drive even affects the way we view the Christian life. We want a "painless Pentecost"; we want a "laughing" re-vival. We want gain without pain; we want the resurrection without going through the grave; we want life without experiencing death; we want a crown without going by way of the cross. But in God's economy, the way up is down.

You and I will never meet God in revival until we first meet Him in brokenness. Our families will never be whole until husbands and wives, moms and dads, and young people have been broken. Our churches will never be the vibrant witness God intended them to be in the world until their members—pastors and laypeople alike —have experienced true brokenness.

That is the heart of what we read about in the book of James:

> *Draw near to God and He will draw near to you. Cleanse your hands, you sinners; and purify your hearts, you double-minded. Lament and mourn and weep! Let your laughter be turned to mourning and your joy to gloom. Humble yourselves in the sight of the Lord, and He will lift you up.*
>
> —James 4:8–10

This is a message today's men and women are not eager to hear. Most of us don't walk into a Christian bookstore and say, "Can you help me find a book on how to 'mourn and weep'?" We want to know how to be happy and whole, how to improve our self-esteem, how to feel better about ourselves and our lives. We think our problem is that we are gloomy and depressed and we need someone to make us happy. But God's Word says, "No, before you can get close to God, you have to find the highway of lowliness."

We want to lift ourselves up. He says, "No, humble yourself, and I will lift you up."

MISCONCEPTIONS ABOUT BROKENNESS

I believe one of the reasons many believers are afraid of the idea of brokenness is that they have misconceptions about what brokenness really means. As is true in so many other areas, our idea of brokenness and God's idea of brokenness are usually quite different.

For example, some people think of brokenness as always being sad or gloomy. They assume it means having a downcast countenance. They imagine that broken people never smile or laugh. How could a broken person possibly be happy or at peace? In reality brokenness brings a release, which produces a deep sense of joy and peace.

Others think of brokenness as being morbidly introspective: "Oh, woe is me! I've confessed every sin I can possibly think of; but surely there must be something I've missed. Oh, what a worm I am!" This kind of "confession" can lead to false humility, wherein people are quick to put themselves down and cannot receive genuine affirmation or encouragement. False humility and morbid introspection are, in fact, the opposite of brokenness, as they reveal a pre-occupation with self, rather than Christ.

For many, brokenness conjures up the image of the shedding of tears—having a deeply emotional experience. They think of a time when they were deeply stirred by a song, moved by a message, or touched by an experience. Unfortunately, countless people have shed buckets full of tears and yet have never experienced a moment of true brokenness. It is difficult to conceive of being truly broken without our emotions being involved. But it is important to understand that it is possible to shed tears without being broken, and it is possible to experience brokenness without shedding any tears at all.

HOW IS BROKENNESS TO BE RECOGNIZED IN OUR LIVES?

Many people equate brokenness with being deeply hurt by tragic circumstances—by the failure of a child, a financial reversal, or perhaps a debilitating illness or death of a loved one.

God often uses tragedy to get people's attention and turn their hearts toward Him. But tragedy doesn't guarantee brokenness. You may have experienced many deep hurts and tragedies and never yet been truly broken.

So what is true brokenness? Someone has said that brokenness, like a fragrance, is easier to detect than to define. How is brokenness to be recognized in our lives?

TRUE BROKENNESS

Brokenness is not a feeling or an emotion. Rather, it requires a choice, an act of the will. Further, this choice is not primarily a one-time experience, though there may be profound and life-changing spiritual turning points in our lives. True brokenness is an ongoing, constant way of life. True brokenness is a lifestyle—a moment-by-moment lifestyle of agreeing with God about the true condition of my heart and life—not as everyone else thinks it is but as He knows it to be.

Brokenness is the shattering of my self-will—the absolute surrender of my will to the will of God.

It is saying "Yes, Lord!"—no resistance, no chafing, no stubbornness—simply submitting myself to His direction and will in my life.

Contrite is one word that is used in the Old Testament to speak of brokenness. That word suggests something that is crushed into small particles or ground into powder, as a rock is pulverized. What is it that God wants to pulverize in us? It is not our spirit He wants to break, nor is it our essential personhood. He wants to break our self-will.

> THE BROKEN, CONTRITE HEART IS EASILY MOLDED BY THE HAND OF GOD.

When we speak of a stallion being "broken," we don't mean that someone physically breaks its legs; we mean that the horse's *will* has been broken—that it is now compliant and submissive to the wishes of its rider. In the same sense, true brokenness is the breaking of my self-will, so that the life and spirit of the Lord Jesus may be released through me. It is my humble and obedient response to the conviction of God's Word and His Holy Spirit.

Brokenness is the stripping of self-reliance and

independence from God. The broken person has no confidence in his own righteousness or his own works, but he is cast in total dependence upon the grace of God working in and through him.

Brokenness is the softening of the soil of my heart —it is the breaking up of any clods of resistance that could keep the seed from penetrating and taking root. I believe one of the reasons many pastors faithfully preach the Word week after week and see so little fruit in the lives of their listeners is that the soil in many of our hearts has become so hard and fallow that the seed cannot penetrate. Believers with broken, contrite hearts are receptive and responsive to the Word.

As wax or clay must be soft and pliable in order to be molded by the artist's hands, so the broken, contrite heart is easily molded by the hand of God and does not harden itself against the circumstances God chooses to mold it.

ROOF OFF, WALLS DOWN

In 1 John, the apostle explains that our relationship with God is inseparably linked to our relationship with other believers. He wrote, "If we walk in the light as He is in the light, we have fellowship with one another, and the blood of Jesus Christ His Son cleanses us from all sin" (1 John 1:7). Brokenness in the life of a believer has both a vertical and a horizontal dimension—it goes two ways. First, a broken man or woman walks in transparent honesty and humility before God. That is what it means to "walk in the light." Our lives are open and exposed before the eyes of Him who knows and sees all. Walking in the light means that there is nothing between my soul and my Savior.

However, it is not enough that we be humble and broken before God. Invariably, our relationship with God is reflected in our relationships with others. A person who has been broken before God will also be humble and broken before others. One writer has likened our lives to a house with a roof and walls.[2] For our hearts to be revived, the roof must come off (brokenness toward God) and the walls must come down (brokenness toward man).

I'll never forget listening to one particular man who stood before his fellow staff members as God was moving during the Campus Crusade conference in 1995. As he later recounted in a report to friends and financial supporters, God found this full-time Christian worker in a spiritual drought. During that week, God exposed his heart and took him through a painful process of brokenness that ultimately led to joy and release. That process first required that he let the roof come off in repentance toward God; the process continued and produced rich fruit when he became willing to let the walls down before others. This is what "Jordan" wrote when he looked back on that week:

I showed up at the beginning of the conference with a cold, weary heart. It was difficult for me to sing along with the various praise songs sung during the opening sessions. At times I didn't even try . . . I just listened to everyone else. Friday, Saturday, and Sunday's sessions came and went. Then came Monday.

On Monday morning Nancy addressed the entire staff. In her message, she asked the question, "What kind of heart does God revive?" She contrasted two types of hearts: one being a broken and contrite heart; the other a heart that's full of pride.

What occurred next is something I will remember for the rest of my life. From all across the gymnasium, staff began to make their way to the stage to confess and repent of their sins. A line formed, and for the next thirteen hours there was nonstop public confession. The leadership of our ministry let God move within the hearts of His people and there was true revival!

I had never experienced anything like this before. As I sat in the bleachers, hour after hour, and witnessed fellow staff members weeping in brokenness as they confessed their sin (many times being moved to tears myself by their deep grief), I began to notice God softening my heart as the Holy Spirit began convicting me of my own sin and revealing my need for repentance.

Throughout Monday afternoon I remained in the bleachers and confessed my sin to God, asking Him to forgive me, cleanse me, and create within me a new heart. At first, I didn't believe I needed to go to the microphone. However, by Monday evening, in addition to the sin the Holy Spirit had revealed to me throughout the day,

He had revealed to me some sinful attitudes I needed to confess to my fellow staff. Later that night, at one in the morning, I wrote a four-page letter of confession to God and the staff.

The next day, God gave Jordan the courage to humble himself before the staff and leadership of Campus Crusade, as he read that entire letter publicly and asked for their forgiveness. Jordan's letter was no superficial confession. He made no attempt to whitewash his sins, but brought them out into the light. With his wife standing by his side, he confessed a whole list of specific sins of which God had convicted him: impure motives, a desire for recognition, comparison, caring more about projects and tasks than people, a critical, judgmental spirit, keeping people at arm's length, and a spirit of jealousy and envy. And there was more; he continued reading to the staff what God had put on his heart:

> I am a man of many addictions. Brought up in a home without much nurturing or expressed love, by two people who had their own pain, I

quickly learned how to love myself as a young boy. I loved myself with overeating, then added personal immoral habits, then added spending, and then in college added pornography.

Although I received Christ as a high school student, these addictions followed me into my adult life. Most of my twenties and thirties have been spent in battling these addictive behaviors —each addiction being a form of self-love, each an attempt to mask pain in my life.

Today at the age of thirty-eght, I battle each of these still. I desire victory. I confess each area as sin. Whatever things happened to put these addictions in place don't matter—I'm an adult now and assume full responsibility for their on-going pull and presence in my life.

I also confess to you and the Lord that I have been loving the world and the things of the world more than Him. I have not been experiencing the joy of a close, intimate relationship with God. As a result, my heart has had an emptiness that bass fishing, jazz, chess, and computers simply cannot fill.

I want these things to change. I want repentance. I want brokenness. Please pray that in the

months ahead God will place within me a deep
brokenness and create within me a new, clean
heart—a heart that loves Him more than my
own life.

When he recounted the story later, Jordan
told how those around him extended the grace
and love of God when he allowed the walls of
pride to come down: "Afterward, I was immediately surrounded by over twenty staff members who prayed for me, forgave me, hugged
me, and expressed their love for me. There are
truly very few moments in my life that have
been more meaningful. God is so good. Like the
gracious, loving father of the prodigal son, He
is always ready to restore and welcome His children home."

For Jordan, that initial point of brokenness
was accompanied by a fresh sense of release and
joy in his spirit:

Later that evening, we sang many of the same
songs that were sung the first night of the conference. This time, however, I was singing! And
not just singing, but with a joy in my heart that

I haven't felt for years. As we sang one song entitled "White as Snow," I couldn't help weeping as I experienced the joy of sins forgiven. Much like the sinner woman who couldn't stop weeping at the feet of Jesus, I, too, had been touched by His cleansing love.

He signed his report, "Yielded, broken, and grateful before our gracious, gentle Savior . . ."

About a year later, I had an opportunity to meet Jordan and his wife personally. On a number of occasions since then, I have been able to fellowship with this couple. As painful as it was to expose himself in this way, it was part of the process God used to bring Jordan to a place of newfound freedom and victory. Recently I received a letter from his wife:

Jordan continues to keep his relationship with God fresh and open. He has a goal to read through the Bible this year, and for two years we have faithfully prayed together nightly before we go to sleep. He has kept his commitment to me, to himself, and to the Lord—not flawlessly, but it's our humanness that reminds us both of our never-ending, always present need for the Savior. When failure has happened (which is rare), confession and forgiveness is quickly sought.

Jordan's pathway has not been easy and he has not walked it without some failures along the way. So it will be with anyone who chooses the pathway of brokenness. But as Jordan testifies, the grace of God in his life and in the life of his family has reached beyond anything he'd ever imagined possible. God's richest blessings come only through brokenness. We learn this from our own experiences and from the stories of people like Jordan. And we learn this from the lives of men and women whose encounters with God animate the pages of Scripture.

NOTES

1. Roy Hession, *The Calvary Road* (Fort Washington, Pa.: Christian Literature Crusade, 1990), 21.
2. Norman Grubb, *Continuous Revival* (Fort Washington, Pa.: Christian Literature Crusade, 1997), 15.

3

BIBLICAL PORTRAITS:
BROKEN *and*
UNBROKEN

God creates out of nothing.
Therefore until a man is nothing,
God can make nothing out of him.
—MARTIN LUTHER

Brokenness is not a new idea. From the ancient Hebrew Scriptures to the New Testament, the biblical record provides us with numerous illustrations of people who were broken and humbled before God. Interestingly, these examples are often set in contrast to stories of people who were *not* broken. As we will see, in every case, both individuals sinned. The difference was not so much in the magnitude of their sin but in their response when confronted with their sin.

TWO KINGS

Nearly a thousand years before the birth of Christ, two kings ruled over the nation of Israel. The first king was guilty of what most would consider a few relatively minor infractions. But they cost him his kingdom, his family, and, ultimately, his life.

> BROKEN MEN AND WOMEN HAVE NOTHING TO PROTECT AND NOTHING TO LOSE.

By comparison, his successor was guilty of far greater offenses. In a fit of passion, he committed adultery with his neighbor's wife and then plotted to have his neighbor killed. Yet when the story of his life was told, this man was called "a man after God's own heart" (see 1 Samuel 13:14). What made the difference?

When the first man, King Saul, was confronted with his sin, he defended, justified, and excused himself, blamed others, and tried to cover up both the sin and its consequences. Although he finally admitted, "I have sinned," when caught red-handed by the prophet Samuel, the true condition of Saul's heart was revealed in his next words: "Please don't tell the people!" (see 1 Samuel 15:30). King Saul was more concerned about preserving his reputation and his position—about *looking* good—than about being right with God. His response to God's prophet revealed a proud, unbroken heart.

On the other hand, when King David was faced with his sin, he was willing to acknowledge his failure, to take personal responsibility for his wrongdoing, and to confess and repent of his sin. The roof came off as he repented toward God. The walls came down as he penned two songs of contrition—Psalm 32 and Psalm 51—humbling himself before countless future believers who would read his confession and learn of his failure.

Broken men and women don't care who finds out about their sin; they have nothing to protect and nothing to lose. They are eager for God to be vindicated. David's response when confronted with his wrongdoing was that of a humble, broken man. And his was the heart that God honored. Again and again, God's Word reveals that He is not as concerned about the depth or extent of the sin we commit as He is about our attitude and response when we are confronted with our sin.

STORIES OF PHARISEES AND OTHER SINNERS

In the Gospel of Luke, we find three vivid illustrations of the contrast between a broken person and a proud, unbroken person. Interestingly, in each case, proud people are linked with Pharisees. Now when you and I think of Pharisees, we think of the "bad guys." But in those days, the Pharisees were considered the "good guys." These were the seminary graduates, the biblical scholars, the pastors, the spiritual leaders of their day. Everyone looked up to them; no one questioned their spirituality or their authority. And no one felt that he could possibly measure up to them. It was assumed that the Pharisees were closer to God than anyone else.

When Jesus came along, He stripped away the theological aura the Pharisees had carefully wrapped around themselves. He probed deeply, past their external appearance and acts of apparent devotion, right into the heart where only God can see. Over and over again, He exposed the proud, self-righteous attitudes and motives of the Pharisees and insisted that God rejects that kind of heart. By contrast, He pointed to lowly sinners who had been rejected by everyone else but had repentant hearts. Then and now, broken sinners are the kind of people God chooses to save, to bless, and to help.

TWO WHO PRAYED

In Luke 18, Jesus told a parable about two men who went into the temple to pray. Both were involved in spiritual activity. But one man's prayer was acceptable to God and the other man's prayer didn't make it past the roof. What made the difference? Once again, it was not the outward actions of the men but the condition of their hearts.

The first man, while making an outward show and pretense of piety, was not a true worshiper of God (though he had everyone fooled, including himself). In reality, he worshiped himself; his world revolved around himself. The

Scripture says, "The Pharisee stood and prayed thus *with* [*to;* marginal note NIV] *himself*" (verse 11, italics added). Though his remarks were addressed to God, apparently God wasn't paying much attention as this proud religious leader paraded his spiritual credentials: "God, I thank You that I am not like other men—extortioners, unjust, adulterers, or even as this tax collector. I fast twice a week; I give tithes of all that I possess" (verses 11–12).

Pride led this so-called worshiper to compare himself favorably to other "sinners." It made him utterly blind to his condition and oblivious to the depravity of his own heart.

The other man—a low-down, despised tax collector, who made his living through extortion—apparently had experienced a change of heart. No one needed to tell him he was a sinner. He knew that he had no right to ask or expect anything from God. He could not even bring himself to lift up his eyes to heaven. His eyes downcast, in brokenness and anguish of soul, he simply cried out, "God, be merciful to me a sinner!" (verse 13). This man did not attempt to justify himself; rather, he justified God and recognized that his only hope was if God would have mercy on him.

There is no question about the audience Jesus was trying to reach with this story: "[Jesus] spoke this parable to some who trusted in themselves that they were righteous, and despised others" (verse 9). Jesus intended to be direct; He intended for His story to penetrate and expose the hearts of the proud and unbroken.

You can imagine how uncomfortable and indignant those self-righteous Pharisees must have felt. Could it be that Jesus thought the tax collectors were more righteous before God than they were? Jesus' conclusion to the parable brought the point home even further: "Everyone who exalts himself will be humbled [*put down*; marginal note NKJV], and he who humbles himself will be exalted" (verse 14).

The Pharisees had impressed men with their righteous appearance and their public religious acts, but God was not impressed at all. It is in His very nature to be repulsed by pride and to draw near to those who have a humble, broken spirit.

TWO PEOPLE AT A BANQUET

In the seventh chapter of Luke's Gospel, we read about Jesus being invited for dinner at the home of a Pharisee named Simon. The first verse of this passage gives a glimpse into the heart of this Pharisee: "One of the Pharisees *asked* Him to eat with him" (verse 36, italics added). In the original language, the verb translated "asked" is used in a form that would ordinarily be used to make a request of a peer, rather than the form that would be used to ask a favor of a superior. Simon the Pharisee saw himself being of equal stature with Jesus.

We don't know who else was on the list of invited guests for this dinner, but we do know that one woman came to the dinner without being invited. We are not told her name. We only know that she was a "woman in the city who was a sinner" (verse 37). The implication is that she was a woman of ill repute, a woman with a reputation for sexual promiscuity. She certainly would not have been welcomed at this social gathering by anyone other than Jesus, who gladly welcomes sinners who recognize their need for mercy.

As I have studied this passage and those that parallel it in the synoptic Gospels, I have come to believe that this woman had recently encountered Jesus. Before this occasion, she had responded to His call to repentance, turned from her sin, and embraced Him as the Messiah. He, in turn, had forgiven her and set her free from her sin. Now this newly forgiven woman was returning to Jesus to say "Thank You!" She wanted to express her profound gratitude and love for this One who had transformed her life.

Bearing an alabaster flask of costly perfume, she stood behind the feet of Jesus as He lay reclining at dinner, according to the custom of the day. As she stood quietly in His presence, she began to weep. Now I don't believe this woman came into this dinner intending to be noticed or to make a scene. I don't think she planned to draw attention to herself at all. Instead, she was probably oblivious to the fact that anyone besides Jesus was in that room. She was so overcome with the realization of how Jesus had found her and what He had done for her that she couldn't restrain her spontaneous display of emotion.

Tears of sincere gratitude coursed down her cheeks and onto the Savior's feet. Almost as if she was embarrassed, she stooped and began to wipe the tears off His feet with her hair. This was a picture of the forgiveness she had experienced, for Jesus had wiped her sinful heart clean. Then, presumably stooping even lower, she began to kiss His feet and to anoint them with the perfumed oil she had brought with her. Who better could she lavish this precious substance on than the Son of Man who had delivered her from herself and her sin? Spontaneous and blissfully unself-conscious worship and adoration flowed out of the life of this broken, contrite, forgiven woman.

By contrast, Simon the Pharisee, who had hosted this dinner, was incensed. In his self-righteous state of mind, this woman's behavior and indeed her very presence seemed utterly inappropriate to him. But, of course, Simon's real complaint was not with the woman but with Jesus. Muttering to himself, he said, "This man, if He were a prophet, would know who and what manner of woman this is who is touching Him, for she is a sinner" (Luke 7:39).

Not only did Jesus know what kind of woman she was, He also knew what kind of man Simon was. Further, He knew exactly what Simon was thinking. Jesus spoke to him, "Simon, I have something to say to you." Simon responded, "Teacher, say it."

Jesus proceeded to tell a story about two men who owed a debt to a moneylender. One of the men owed an exorbitant amount—more than he ever could have repaid. The other owed just a paltry sum, but he, too, was without the resources to pay even that small amount. The moneylender "freely forgave them both." Now Jesus said, "Tell Me, which of them will love the moneylender more?"

Simon correctly answered, "The one who was forgiven the bigger debt."

"You're right," said Jesus. Then, to help Simon apply the word picture, He reminded him of what had just taken place in Simon's own home. Simon had not treated Jesus with even common courtesy, much less the respect that would normally be shown a guest of honor. He had not provided water to wash His feet, he had not greeted Jesus with a kiss (equal to a handshake in our day), and he had not offered oil to anoint Jesus' head.

The woman, on the other hand, though an outcast and tainted by past failure and shame, had washed Jesus' feet with her tears and wiped them with the hair of her head. She had kissed His feet and anointed them with oil.

According to Jesus, because this woman had been forgiven of such serious sin, she felt herself to be a great debtor and therefore loved Jesus greatly. It wasn't that Simon's need for forgiveness was any less than hers. However, in the blind arrogance of his heart, he simply didn't realize how great a sinner he was, nor how great was his need for forgiveness. Consequently, he was not able to express the kind of worship and love that this woman had lavished on Jesus.

As I reread this passage, I have to acknowledge that my own relationship and responses to the Lord Jesus often resemble Simon's more than that of the "sinner woman." I am grieved by the coldness, indifference, and hardness of my heart toward the Savior; I long to be able to express that spontaneous, extravagant love and devotion that pours forth out of a broken, contrite heart—a heart that recognizes the greatness of my sin and the surpassing greatness of His grace.

TWO SONS AND THEIR FATHER

When the scene opens in Luke chapter 15, we find two kinds of people in the audience: "Then all the *tax collectors and the sinners* drew near to Him to hear Him. And the *Pharisees and scribes* complained, saying, 'This Man receives sinners and eats with them.' So He spoke this parable to them . . ." (verses 1–3, italics added).

As was generally the case, some in the crowd were all too aware that they were sinners, and they were drawn like a magnet to Jesus and His teaching. They hung on Jesus' every word, for His message was their only hope. Meanwhile, there was another group over on the sidelines. Although these religious men were equally sinful, they did not see themselves as such. Instead, they did what proud, unbroken people usually do when confronted with the truth:

They criticized and picked apart the message and the messenger: "*Can you believe it*—this man welcomes *sinners!* He even *eats* with them!" They not only failed to see themselves as sinners in need of God's grace, but they also despised others and couldn't bear the thought of guilt by association with those whom they thought of as common, ordinary sinners. These prideful religious characters kept their distance from everybody else.

In an effort to expose their proud, self-righteous hearts, Jesus told three stories. He spoke first of the lost sheep, then of the lost coin, and finally He told the familiar story of the lost son.

Actually, there were two lost sons in this story—two young men whose responses revealed the true condition of their hearts. The younger son, commonly called "the Prodigal Son," abused his family name and squandered his inheritance. Finally, having lost it all, he woke up to what he had done and where it had led him.

Alone and poverty-stricken, he was truly broken. Realizing that he had nowhere else to turn, he made a decision to repent; he chose the pathway of brokenness and humility. He made the tough choice to return to the place where his failure had begun and to be reconciled with those he had wronged.

For this broken, repentant son there was no self-justification, no trivializing of his behavior, no whitewashing of his sin, no making excuses, no blaming others, no expectation of being treated royally. He knew he had nothing to offer but an honest acknowledgment of his failure and a humble plea for mercy.

The response of the boy's father is a powerful and poignant picture of our heavenly Father's welcome toward us when we come to Him in genuine repentance. This called for a celebration—the once-haughty rebel had returned home as a broken and humble repenter.

It's a great story with a great ending.

But remember that there were two types of people in the crowd that day. The tax collectors and sinners had to love this story—it spoke of hope, of forgiveness, of mercy. But what about the Pharisees and scribes? What were they thinking? Did they find it hard to swallow such a generous display of grace for one so undeserving?

Did they find themselves looking around to see to whom this story could possibly apply?

Jesus wasn't finished. Just as there were two kinds of people listening, there were also two sons in the story. Where was the Prodigal's older brother while all the partying was going on? He was, of course, right where he was supposed to be —out in the field, being faithful, working hard, doing his job. Here we encounter a stereotypical obedient, compliant, respectable firstborn. I should know; I'm one too.

This son had never given his father a moment's grief, especially not when compared with his free-spirited sibling. He had never been rebellious, at least not outwardly. But God is not impressed with outward appearances; He looks into the *heart*. And a celebration surrounding a repentant brother's return was the perfect setting in which to expose the elder brother's motives and attitudes.

As the older son approached his house, he heard, of all things, music and dancing. What in the world was going on? There hadn't been a party around that place since his rebellious younger brother left home. Rather than going to his father (could this suggest that although he was a "model son," he didn't have much of a relationship with his dad?), he found a servant and asked, "What's going on?"

The servant gave him the bottom line, "Your brother has returned home and your dad is throwing a party." The servant, unfortunately, failed to mention the heart of the matter—the younger brother's transformation into a contrite, humble son.

Now the older boy's real nature began to be exposed: "He was angry and would not go in" (verse 28). How typical this is of proud, unbroken people. They cannot rejoice over repentant sinners. They are consumed with a sense of their own rights and expectations. And if they don't get the treatment they feel they deserve, they throw a pity party for themselves.

In the midst of celebrating the return of his lost son, news of his older son's boycott reached the father. He immediately left the party to deal with another troubled offspring.

I understand that in the ancient Jewish culture, when the head of the home left the party, the music and the dancing stopped until the host returned. Isn't that a picture of what is happening in so many of our churches and ministries today? There's no joy, no celebration, no partying over lost sinners being restored, because the pastor and the leadership are so distracted with having to deal with petty, pouting "Pharisees" ("elder brothers") who are throwing fits because they didn't get their way.

The pride, self-righteousness, and blindness of the older son's heart finally came to the surface in his angry, accusatory speech to his dad: "Lo, these many years I have been serving you [what was his motive for serving?]; I never transgressed your commandment at any time [was he really that perfect?]; and yet you never gave me a young goat, that I might make merry with my friends [what ingratitude—at least half the inheritance was already his]. But as soon as this son of yours came [not *my brother* but *your son*], who has devoured your livelihood with harlots [says who? he assumes the

> DO WE FAIL TO RECOGNIZE THE "ELDER BROTHER" WHEN HE IS STARING BACK AT US IN THE MIRROR?

worst], you killed the fatted calf for him'" (verses 29–30).

Buried beneath the older son's seemingly perfect exterior lay a dark, cancerous mass of anger, rebellion, and envy, fueled by hidden, unfulfilled expectations. This young man had an inflated sense of his own worth and a secret desire for recognition that surfaced when someone he deemed less worthy than himself became a recipient of lavish grace.

The application of this story to the Pharisees who were seated in the crowd that day seems obvious to us. But I wonder if it was obvious to them. Or were they so blinded by their pride that they couldn't see that Jesus' description of the elder brother fit them perfectly? And could we be so blind to our own need that we fail to recognize the "elder brother" when he is staring back at us in the mirror?

BROKEN OR UNBROKEN?

We've reflected upon four biblical accounts. We've seen four individuals who were humble and broken, and four people or groups of people who were proud and unbroken. Is it merely co-incidental that in all four cases, the proud people were respected individuals who held an elevated position or had some sort of leadership responsibility?

The fact is, the higher up we find ourselves in terms of power, influence, and wealth—the more people look up to us—the more vulnerable we are to pride and self-deceit, and the more prone we are to be blind to our spiritual needs and deficiencies. Once we are established in a position of influence, we have a reputation to maintain. We have a lot to lose if we get honest about our real spiritual needs. For most of us, the subtle encroachment of pride is more dangerous, and more likely to render us useless to God and others, than any other kind of failure.

> WE MAY BE MISSING THE HEART OF THE GOSPEL AND THE GRACE OF CHRIST.

As you consider these four comparisons between proud and broken people, with which of those characters do you most identify? Do you relate to adulterous King David? To the cheating tax collector? To the sexually promiscuous woman? To the lustful, wild-living Prodigal? "No way," you say. "I'd never do anything like that!"

Well, then, do you relate to proud King Saul? To the self-righteous Pharisees? To the angry elder brother?

And, by the way, with which of these kinds of individuals do you think Jesus was most comfortable? Though it seemed scandalous and outrageous to the Pharisees of His day, as it does to modern-day Pharisees, Jesus was always drawn to those whose sin seemed to be more egregious (from a human point of view), but who were repentant over their sin. On the other hand, He was repulsed by those who looked like perfect saints but whose hearts were proud and unbroken.

Could it be that God is more offended by those of us who appear to be respectable and spiritual but who have proud, unteachable spirits, than He is by adulterers, fornicators, sodomites, abortionists, or pornographers who make no pretense of being godly? The sobering reality is that proud, unbroken Christians have done far more damage to the church of Jesus Christ than any sinners outside the church could inflict.

In our focus on the needs and failures of those we consider less spiritual than ourselves, and in our drive to perform and to protect our image, we may be missing the heart of the Gospel and the grace of Christ.

You see, the message of repentance is not just for adulterers and prodigals; it is also for elder brothers and Pharisees and respected leaders. The Good News is that, regardless of which category we may find ourselves in, the grace of God is always available to those who lay down their pride and offer the sacrifice of a broken, contrite heart.

4
AM I A PROUD
or a
BROKEN PERSON?

*Pride is the greatest of all evils that beset us,
and of all our enemies it is
that which dies the slowest and hardest.*

—J. N. DARBY[1]

Years ago a missionary served in a region in Africa that had known seasons of true revival. He reported that whenever he would mention the name of any Christian, the national believers would ask him, "Is he a broken Christian?" They did not ask, "Is he a committed Christian?" or "Is he a knowledgeable Christian?" or "Is he a hardworking Christian?" They wanted to know, "Is he a broken Christian?"

Are you a broken Christian? Am I? How can we know?

Over the years I have asked the Lord to show me some of the characteristics of a broken person, and how they compare with a person with a proud spirit. In the form of a "proud versus broken" comparison, I have listed some of the things that have come to my attention as I've allowed the Lord to search my own heart. This is by no means an exhaustive list; the Lord will undoubtedly show you other characteristics as you open your heart to Him.

Let me encourage you to avoid the temptation to skim through this list. Instead, take time to read it prayerfully and ask God to show you, "Am I a proud or a broken person?" You may even want to place a small check mark next to any evidences of pride that you see in your life. That simple act could be an important step toward cultivating the broken, humble heart that God revives.

ATTITUDES TOWARD OTHERS

⟋ 1. Proud people focus on the failures of others and can readily point out those faults.

Broken people are more conscious of their own spiritual need than of anyone else's.

◦ 2. Proud people have a critical, faultfinding spirit. They look at everyone else's faults with a microscope but view their own with a telescope.

Broken people are compassionate—they have the kind of love that overlooks a multitude of sins; they can forgive much because they know how much they have been forgiven.

◦ 3. Proud people are especially prone to criticize those in positions of authority— their pastor, their boss, their husband, their parents—and they talk to others about the faults they see.

Broken people reverence, encourage, and lift up those that God has placed in positions of authority, and they talk to God in intercession, rather than gossiping about the faults they see in others.

⟞ 4. Proud people are self-righteous; they think highly of themselves and look down on others.

Broken people think the best of others; they esteem others as better than themselves.

⟞ 5. Proud people have an independent, self-sufficient spirit.

Broken people have a dependent spirit; they recognize their need for God and for others.

ATTITUDES ABOUT RIGHTS

⟞ 6. Proud people have to prove that they are right—they have to get the last word.

Broken people are willing to yield the right to be right.

⟞ 7. Proud people claim rights and have a demanding spirit.

Broken people yield their rights and have a meek spirit.

⤳ 8. Proud people are self-protective of their time, their rights, and their reputation.

Broken people are self-denying and self-sacrificing.

ATTITUDES ABOUT SERVICE AND MINISTRY

⤳ 9. Proud people desire to be served— they want life to revolve around them and their own needs.

Broken people are motivated to serve others and to be sure others' needs are met before their own.

⤳ 10. Proud people desire to be known as a success.

Broken people are motivated to be faithful and to make others successful.

⤳ 11. Proud people have a feeling— conscious or subconscious—that "this

ministry (or this organization) is privileged
to have me and my gifts." They focus on
what they can do for God.

*Broken people have a heart attitude that says,
"I don't deserve to have any part in this ministry"; they know that they have nothing to offer
God except the life of Jesus flowing through
their broken lives.*

ATTITUDES ABOUT RECOGNITION

12. Proud people crave self-advancement.

Broken people desire to promote others.

13. Proud people have a drive to be recognized and appreciated for their efforts.

*Broken people have a sense of their own unwor-
thiness; they are thrilled that God would use
them at all.*

14. Proud people get wounded when others are promoted and they are overlooked.

Broken people are eager for others to get the credit, and they rejoice when others are lifted up.

⟿ 15. Proud people are elated by praise and deflated by criticism.

Broken people know that any praise of their accomplishments belongs to the Lord and that criticism can help them grow into spiritual maturity.

ATTITUDES ABOUT THEMSELVES

⟿ 16. Proud people feel confident in how much they know.

Broken people are humbled by how very much they have to learn.

⟿ 17. Proud people are self-conscious; they worry about what others think of them.

Broken people are not preoccupied with what others think of them.

⟋ 18. Proud people are concerned about appearing respectable; they are driven to protect their image and reputation.

Broken people are concerned with being real; they care less about what others think than about what God knows—they are willing to die to their own reputation.

⟋ 19. Proud people can't bear to fail or for anyone to think they are less than perfect. This can drive them to extremes—workaholic tendencies, perfectionism, the tendency to drive others or to place unrealistic expectations on themselves or others.

Broken people can recognize and live within God-given limitations.

ATTITUDES ABOUT RELATIONSHIPS

⟋ 20. Proud people keep others at arm's length.

Broken people are willing to take the risks of getting close to others and loving intimately.

‿ 21. Proud people are quick to blame others.

Broken people accept personal responsibility and can acknowledge where they were wrong in a situation.

‿ 22. Proud people wait for others to come and ask forgiveness when there is a misunderstanding or a breach in a relationship.

Broken people take the initiative to be reconciled, no matter how wrong the other party may have been.

‿ 23. Proud people are unapproachable or defensive when corrected.

Broken people receive correction with a humble, open spirit.

24. Proud people find it difficult to discuss their spiritual needs with others.

Broken people are willing to be open and transparent with others as God directs.

25. Proud people try to control the people and the circumstances around them— they are prone to manipulate.

Broken people trust in God—they rest in Him and are able to wait for Him to act on their behalf.

26. Proud people become bitter and resentful when they are wronged; they have emotional temper tantrums; they hold others hostage and are easily offended; they carry grudges and keep a record of others' wrongs.

Broken people give thanks in all things; they are quick to forgive those who wrong them.

ATTITUDES ABOUT SIN

 27. Proud people want to be sure that no one finds out when they have sinned; their instinct is to cover up.

Broken people aren't overly concerned with who knows or who finds out about their sin—they are willing to be exposed because they have nothing to lose.

 28. Proud people have a hard time saying, "I was wrong; will you please forgive me?"

Broken people are quick to admit their failure and to seek forgiveness when necessary.

 29. Proud people tend to deal in generalities when confessing their sin to God ("Dear Lord, please forgive me for all my sins . . .") or expressing spiritual need to others ("I need to be a better Christian . . .").

Broken people are able to acknowledge specifics when confessing their sin: "Lord, I agree with You that I love myself more than I love my mate; I confess that I am addicted to television; I'm a glutton; I have a critical spirit; I am an angry mother. . . ."

⟳ 30. Proud people are concerned about the consequences of their sin. They are disturbed over the problems caused by their sin—for example, the financial bondage created by their overspending, or the problems in their marriage that have resulted from selfishness and immoral choices.

Broken people are grieved over the cause, the root of their sin. They are more concerned about how their sin has grieved and dishonored God than about the problems it has created in their lives.

⟳ 31. Proud people are remorseful over their sin—sorry that they got caught or found out.

Broken people are truly repentant over their sin, and the evidence of their repentance is that they forsake the sin.

ATTITUDES ABOUT THEIR WALK WITH GOD

32. Proud people are blind to the true condition of their hearts.

Broken people walk in the light and acknowledge the truth about their lives.

33. Proud people compare themselves with others and feel worthy of respect.

Broken people compare themselves with the holiness of God and feel a desperate need for His mercy.

34. Proud people don't think they need to repent of anything.

Broken people realize that they need to maintain a continual heart attitude of repentance.

⌒ 35. Proud people don't think they need revival, but they are sure everyone else does. (In fact, right about now, they are making a mental list of the people they think need to read this book!)

Broken people continually sense their need for a fresh encounter with God and for a fresh filling of His Holy Spirit.[2]

Are you a "broken Christian"? Based on these characteristics, how would you answer that question? How would those in your family or your workplace respond if they were asked, "Is he/she a broken Christian?" Most important, what would God say?

If this list has helped you realize that you are a proud, rather than a broken, person, do not despair. God has been merciful to show you your need. The first step to brokenness and humility is to get honest and acknowledge your need. Walk in the light; agree with God about what He has revealed to be the true condition of your heart. Don't try to cover up, justify, rationalize, compare yourself with your mate, or pretend that you are better off than you really are. "Humble [yourself] in the sight of the Lord, and He will lift you up" (James 4:10). The infinite riches and blessings of the kingdom of God belong to those who recognize their spiritual poverty.

NOTES

1. Edwin and Lillian Harvey, comps., *Royal Insignia* (Yanceyville, N.C.: Harvey & Tait, 1992), 87.
2. The key points from this list are available on a bookmark (individually or in quantity). Contact Revive Our Hearts, P.O. Box 31, Buchanan, MI 49107; (269) 684-5905; e-mail: Info@LifeAction.org.

5

THE BLESSING
of
BROKENNESS

The broken person . . .
will find that all of the resources of heaven
and all of the Spirit's power are now at his disposal
and, unless heaven's riches can be exhausted
or the Spirit's power can be found wanting,
he cannot come up short.

—JENNIFER KENNEDY DEAN[1]

By most standards, Brian and Melanie Adams had a good marriage. They were both believers, they were committed to each other, and they were trying to lead their eight children to follow Christ. However, over nineteen years of marriage, the intimacy they had once experienced had gradually eroded. Melanie says, "The dinner table had grown larger and larger between us with the addition of each child, and I had almost come to accept that we would never experience the closeness that we both longed for and needed."

When they had an opportunity to attend a retreat called "Renewing Your Heart—Reviving Your Marriage," Melanie hoped this might be just what they needed. In her "humble" opinion, her husband needed to improve in some areas, and what better place to repair your husband than a marriage retreat!

On the second day of the retreat, the speaker gave a message on bitterness and the need for personal brokenness and humility. As Melanie and Brian walked back to their room together following the session, Melanie was mentally preparing a lecture for Brian on the need for brokenness in his life.

What followed can only be described as a supernatural work of the Spirit in Melanie's heart. She writes: "God began to peel back the layers of my heart, and what was revealed was not pretty: bitterness, hardness of heart, hate, rebellion, and most of all a dependence on my own righteousness, and an underlying pride that corrupted all."

As God showed Melanie the true condition

of her heart, she began to cry, then to weep. Sobs of grief and despair racked her body. Her shocked husband held her close as she poured out her confession. Like an infection being drained from a lanced cyst, the pride and self-righteousness were purged from her spirit.

WHAT KINDS OF
BLESSINGS DOES
BROKENNESS
BRING?

From that place of humility and brokenness before God and her husband, Melanie cried out to God to take away her heart of stone and give her a heart of flesh. She describes what happened next: "In His mercy, like a refreshing, cleansing wind, the Spirit of God swept through my heart. My tears of anguish were transformed to tears of joy, forgiveness, and freedom. God had chosen to reveal His glory—and I will never be the same. Never."

Why would anyone choose to be broken? Well, why would a man check into a hospital and allow the surgeon to start cutting? Is it because he loves pain? Of course not. It is because he knows that surgery is the only way to experience healing and to be physically restored.

What makes a woman willing to endure long hours of intense labor? She knows that beyond the labor there will be the joy of a new life.

So why would anyone choose the pathway of brokenness? Because, as Melanie discovered, *brokenness brings blessedness.* Jesus said, *"Blessed are the poor in spirit"*—contrary to what we would expect, brokenness is the pathway to blessing! There are no alternate routes; there are no shortcuts. The very thing we dread and are tempted to resist is actually the means to God's greatest blessings in our lives. What kinds of blessings does brokenness bring?

GOD DRAWS NEAR TO THE BROKEN

Again and again in the Scripture, we learn that God "resists the proud" (Proverbs 3:34; James 4:6; 1 Peter 5:5). The concept here is that God sets Himself in "battle array" against those who are proud; He stiff-arms the arrogant; He keeps them at a distance. God repels those who are self-sufficient and who take unholy pride in their accomplishments.

On the other hand, He pours grace on the

humble. He comes to the rescue of the humble. Like an ambulance racing to the scene in response to a call for help, so God races to the scene when His children humble themselves and acknowledge their need. As Charles Spurgeon reminds us, "He that humbles himself under the hand of God shall not fail to be enriched, uplifted, sustained, and comforted by the ever-gracious One. It is a habit of Jehovah to cast down the proud, and lift up the lowly."[2]

Over and over again, I have experienced the grace of God poured out in response to my need. I recall one particular day when I found myself physically and emotionally depleted in the midst of an especially grueling season of ministry. I was getting ready to leave on yet another trip when I "hit the wall," feeling that I just could not go on. I collapsed into a chair in my study and began to sob uncontrollably. At that point, I had two options. I could try to pull myself together, put on a strong front, put one foot in front of the other, and somehow muster up the strength to do what I had to do.

However, I knew that acting in self-sufficiency would cause me to forfeit the grace and presence of God in my life. I knew how much I needed His grace, and I could not bear the thought of going on without His presence. So in my weakness and desperation, I chose option two: I made the conscious decision to humble myself, to acknowledge my need, and to cry out to the Lord for grace. After praying and confirming that He indeed wanted me to make the trip, I asked Him for the supernatural enabling to do what He had called me to do.

The next day I stood and addressed an audience of full-time Christian workers. My topic was "The Potential Pitfalls of Ministry." The reality was, at the time, that I had fallen into or was perilously close to several of those pitfalls myself. I was tempted to try to protect my image before those Christian workers—to leave them with the impression that I had somehow avoided all those pitfalls and that *they* were the ones who needed this message.

But I knew that *I* was the one who really needed that message, and that if I wanted God's grace to meet me at my point of need, I needed to humble myself before Him (roof off) and before those in the audience (walls down) and be honest about the condition of my own life.

Do you wonder why God sometimes seems so far away? Could it be that He has withdrawn His presence and is resisting you because of lingering pride in your heart? "Though the Lord is on high, yet He regards the lowly; but the proud He knows from afar" (Psalm 138:6).

> THIS MYSTERY IS THAT *DEATH BRINGS LIFE.*

Do you want to be close to God? Even as the father of the Prodigal Son drew his broken, repentant boy to his chest and embraced and restored him, so our heavenly Father draws near to those who come to Him with humble, broken hearts.

NEW LIFE IS RELEASED

Recently a friend wrote to tell me how God had brought him to a fresh point of brokenness. In describing the difference brokenness has made in his life, he used a vivid word picture:

Prior to this time, I struggled with low-grade depression. I had turned so much anger inward that it had become churning hatred, which affected my entire attitude. However, since God brought me to a new point of brokenness, I have described my life as one that has moved from being in a black and white movie, to being lived in a *full color motion picture!*

My friend's experience illustrates another blessing of brokenness. When we are faced with the prospect of being broken with Christ at the Cross, we are tempted to believe that will be the end for us. And in a sense, it is the end—the end of our pride, our self-life, and the rule of our flesh. But in reality, it is just the beginning. Through our willingness to be united with Christ in His death, new life is released through our brokenness—the supernatural, resurrection life of Christ.

In John 12, immediately following the triumphal entry into Jerusalem, Jesus turned to His disciples and began to speak of His imminent death. He introduced the subject by saying, "The hour has come that the Son of Man should be glorified" (verse 23). Glorified? Why would anyone describe his *death* as the hour in which he would be glorified? Hadn't Jesus just been glorified when He was escorted into Jerusalem by throngs of adoring worshipers?

Jesus understood something that His disciples would not grasp until after His death, resurrection, and ascension back into heaven— something the Bible calls a "mystery." This mystery is that *death brings life,* and that there can be no real life apart from our willingness to die. To help explain this principle, Jesus used an illustration from the world of farming: "Unless a grain of wheat falls into the ground and *dies,* it remains alone; but if it *dies,* it produces much grain" (verse 24, italics added).

I can take a grain of wheat and clean it up, put it on a beautiful piece of china on my dining room table, shine lights on it, play music for it, pray for it, and what will happen to it? Absolutely nothing! It will always just sit there "alone." What has to happen to that grain if it is to bear fruit? It must go down into the ground and *die.* If that grain of wheat had feelings, I can imagine it might say, "Hey, it's dark down here! It's cold down here! It's lonely down here!" But in that dark, cold, lonely place, the grain will shed its hard outer husk so that the life within it may be released. Then—after it has "died"—it will put down roots, and the first shoots of new life will finally spring forth.

By the way, I believe one of the reasons that so many people live with chronic loneliness is that they are unwilling to die. As Jesus pointed out, if a grain of wheat does not fall into the ground and die, it "remains alone." Our natural instinct is to hold on protectively to our own lives. When we refuse to shed that hard, outer shell called "self," no one can get close to us; no one can penetrate or enter into our life. Just as pride repulses God, so pride keeps others from getting close to us.

Years ago, when I was a college student, I heard Pastor Ray Ortlund say, "Most churches are like a bag of marbles—all hard and clanging up against one another. Instead, we ought to be like a bag of grapes—*squished* together so that the juice of His Spirit may flow out through us." True Christian community, as Pastor Ray described it, is something few believers ever experience, because it requires that each individual let go of "self" and pour out his life on behalf of others.

What does this kind of death mean? It means that we must be willing to die to our own interests, die to our own reputation, die to our own rights, die to our own ways of doing things, die to our own comfort, convenience, hopes, dreams, and aspirations. To "die" means to lay it all down. To give it all up. To let it all go. This may seem difficult, perhaps even unthinkable, to our self-protective, individualistic, rights-oriented minds. But, as Jesus went on to tell His disciples, "He who loves his life will lose it, and he who hates his life in this world will keep it for eternal life" (John 12:25).

What was Jesus saying? The only way to gain your life is to give it up. The only way to win it is to lose it. We think we are giving up so much by dying. But in reality, it is those who refuse to die who are giving up everything. When we choose the pathway of brokenness and humility we are choosing to receive new life—His supernatural, abundant life—flowing in us and through us.

Of course, the ultimate picture of that kind of brokenness is the Lord Jesus Himself. He is the One who said, "This is My body which is *broken* for you" (1 Corinthians 11:24, italics added).

THE CROSS BE-
CAME THE SITE
OF CHRIST'S
TRUE GLORIFI-
CATION.

The prophet Isaiah spoke of the Lord Jesus when he said, "He was wounded for our transgressions, He was *bruised* for our iniquities. . . . It pleased the Lord to *bruise* Him" (53:5, 10, italics added).

Interestingly, the word translated *bruised* in Isaiah 53 is a variation of the word used in Isaiah 57:15, where God says, "I dwell . . . with him who has a *contrite* and humble spirit, to revive the spirit of the humble, and to revive the heart of the *contrite* ones." As we have seen, that word means to be crushed or broken in pieces. Jesus was willing to be crushed, to die, so that through His death, eternal life could be released for us.

In both the natural and supernatural realms, *death brings life.* The petals of the rose must be crushed for the perfume to be released, and the caterpillar must die to its life as a caterpillar and surrender to the confines of a chrysalis so it can be metamorphosed into a butterfly. The apostle Paul said that if "the rulers of this age" (including Satan and his demons) had known this mystery, they never would have crucified the Lord Jesus (1 Corinthians 2:8). They thought the Cross was Jesus' ultimate defeat and their final triumph. In fact, it proved to be just the reverse.

Because Jesus understood the ways of God, He did not resent or resist His death. He reminded His disciples that no man took His life from Him, but that He laid it down willingly (John 10:18). When the time came, in obedience to the will of His Father, He turned His face toward Calvary and went as a lamb to the slaughter. He knew that beyond the Cross there was life everlasting. For this reason, the Cross became the site of His true glorification—the place where He conquered death and gave birth to eternal life.

So, too, when you and I are willing to be broken in union with Him, His abundant life is released to flow through us to others. Brokenness is the entrance into life. Not until we are broken can we begin to experience the free flow of the power of His Spirit in and through our lives.

DEEPER LOVE, DEEPER WORSHIP

When Melanie Adams finally came to the end of herself and was broken before God and her husband, God began to increase her capacity for love and for worship. Several months after that initial point of brokenness, Melanie wrote to tell some of the changes that had taken place in her life as a result:

I have fallen in love with my husband more deeply than ever. It was quite a rude awakening to realize the chasm in our marriage was my fault, born of an unforgiving heart. My husband has forgiven me and I smile at the future.

I have developed the somewhat frustrating habit of crying all the time—not a normal response for me. In church, a song of worship or a meaningful message finds me borrowing my husband's handkerchief as he gently pats my hand.

God's Word jumps off the page every time I open His Holy Book—it is personal now. I enjoy a sweet communion with the Lord and have heartfelt gratitude for His love and sacrifice that I never knew before. I have peace and joy, and He has given me a new song.

Like Melanie, the "sinner woman" who anointed Jesus' feet was able to love much because she had been forgiven much. We see in this unnamed woman of Luke 7 a freedom and an abandon that many believers never experience. She was oblivious to the rejection or the disapproval of anyone around her.

WHY IS IT SO HARD FOR US TO EXPRESS OUR LOVE AND WORSHIP?

Her expressions of worship and love were extravagant and lavish. All that mattered to her was Jesus.

Have you ever known someone who worshiped the Lord with great abandon, who was unusually free to express her love to God and to others? Perhaps you envied her freedom. Or perhaps you found yourself feeling critical—

questioning her motives or the appropriateness of her behavior, even as Simon the Pharisee was critical of the woman who "crashed" his dinner party.

So many of us are bound up in our ability to express love and worship. And it's odd, because many of us have no difficulty cheering till we're hoarse at a ball game. But to *sing* aloud in church? To lift our hands in adoration before the Lord? To pray aloud in front of others? To step out of our comfort zone and engage someone we don't know in a spiritual conversation? To express verbal appreciation for what another believer has meant in our life? That's another matter altogether.

Why is it so hard for us to express our love and worship? Perhaps it is because we still have the roof on and the walls up. Pride causes us to erect barriers between ourselves and God and walls between ourselves and others. It makes us so concerned about what others think that we are imprisoned to our inhibitions.

"But that's just my personality—I'm naturally shy," someone might counter. Let's get honest. Is it really a matter of personality, or could it be a matter of pride? When our personality is surrendered to the Holy Spirit, He will express the heart of God in and through us. We will no longer be self-conscious but entirely God-conscious.

There is a lot being said today about freedom, love, and worship, and a fervent attempt is being made in many circles to cultivate love in the body of Christ and create worshipful experiences. However, true freedom, love, and worship cannot be manufactured or engineered. Part of the problem is that we are short-circuiting the process that God has established that leads to these things.

True worship begins with *brokenness and humility* over whatever God reveals to us in His Word. Poverty of spirit and mourning over our sin lead to genuine *repentance,* which in turn leads to *forgiveness.* Forgiveness will produce *freedom*—freedom from guilt and bondage. When we have freedom that has been birthed out of brokenness, repentance, and forgiveness, we will have a greater capacity for *love*—supernatural ability to love God and to love those who are unlovable—and for *worship.* And of course, true love and worship will lead us back to a new level of brokenness, which leads to greater and deeper repentance, increased forgiveness, newfound freedom, and an even greater capacity for love and for worship.

Brokenness is the starting place for a lifelong cycle. We cannot experience true freedom, love, and worship if we do not enter by way of humility, repentance, and forgiveness.

One of the most memorable things to me about the Campus Crusade gathering in 1995 is the obvious way that personal and corporate brokenness resulted in a new capacity for love and worship. Initially, as people began to mourn and grieve over their sin, the atmosphere was heavy, as God's hand of conviction settled in on that auditorium. Nobody felt much like singing. But over the next couple of days, people began to sing—not because a worship leader said it was time to sing but simply out of gratitude and devotion to Jesus. Many of the songs focused on the grace of God and the wonder of His love and forgiveness.

Rarely have I heard more beautiful or heartfelt music than that which poured forth from those freshly cleansed hearts and lives. As the week progressed, the spirit of praise and worship began to intensify. On the final evening of the conference, the celebration was unforgettable. Strains of "Shout to the Lord All the Earth!" nearly lifted the roof off the building.

The night of weeping turned to shouts of joy (Psalm 30:5); the bones that He had broken began to rejoice (Psalm 51:8); hearts that had been delivered from guilt were freed to sing aloud of His righteousness (Psalm 51:14); the spirit of heaviness was replaced with the garment of praise (Isaiah 61:3). So it will be in the lives of all who choose the pathway of brokenness.

ABLE TO BE USED BY GOD

One of the recurring themes of Scripture is that God uses things and people that are broken. That is His way. The turning point of Jacob's life took place in a wrestling match in the middle of the night at the River Jabbok (Genesis 32). Years earlier God had promised to bless Jacob, but he had never been able to enjoy that blessing because he had been trying to control and manage life on his own terms.

Now, at Jabbok, Jacob came to a situation over which he had no control and which he could not manage. The next morning he was to meet his estranged brother who was approaching with an army. Jacob the conniver was cornered, and he was terrified. God had his attention. That night God, in the form of an angel, met Jacob and engaged him in hand-to-hand combat, while Jacob struggled to elicit the blessing that already belonged to him.

> IN CONCEDING DEFEAT, JACOB WON HIS ULTIMATE VICTORY.

The real victory was won when Jacob was overcome by the angel, and when the angel asked Jacob his name. At that moment, I wonder if Jacob had a flashback to the day years earlier when he had been trying to wrest a blessing from his elderly, blind father. Isaac had asked him, "Who are you, my son?" (Genesis 27:18), and Jacob had deceived his father by claiming to be his brother Esau. The pride of his heart had caused him to pretend to be somebody he wasn't.

This time, Jacob had met his match. No longer controlling, he had come under the control of One infinitely stronger than he, and he finally spoke the truth about who he was:

"What is your name?"

"Jacob."

No pretending, no trying to leave a good impression, no explaining, no justifying. Jacob spoke the bare, naked truth. "Jacob—the schemer, the deceiver, the manipulator, the con artist. That's who I am." And in conceding defeat, Jacob won his ultimate victory. At that point, he was a new man. With Jacob's natural strength broken down, God was able to clothe him with spiritual power. Once he admitted the truth about who he was, God gave him a new name—*Israel,* meaning "prince with God"—representative of a new character. Now he was usable in God's hands.

Like Jacob, Moses also knew the power of brokenness. After forty years in the palace where he was part of the royal court, it took forty more years in the desert to strip him of all his natural assets—giftedness, contacts, position, reputation. Moses lost it all. But he emerged at the burning bush a broken man, usable in the hands of God.

When the children of Israel arrived at Mt. Horeb and found no drinking water, Moses got another lesson in brokenness (Exodus 17). "Strike the rock," God said, "and water will come out." Anybody knows you don't get water out of a rock. But obediently, Moses struck the rock—a picture of Christ being smitten, broken for us—and water came gushing out to quench the thirst of two million thirsty Israelites in the desert.

And then there was the unlikely military leader named Gideon. Hopelessly outnumbered by the Midianite army, Gideon's ragtag assortment of soldiers had no chance of survival, much less of victory. But as is so often the case, brokenness was the name of God's battle plan. Break down the army until there are so few that you look ridiculous. Break the pitchers so that the light of the lanterns within can shine forth. Out of brokenness comes light, and in that light the enemy is thrown into disarray, the victory is won. In the end, everyone knows Who won the battle.

Our greatest example, of course, is the Lord
Jesus. When His body was broken on Calvary,
eternal life was released for the salvation of the
world. Do you want to live a fruitful life? Do
you want the fragrance of the life of Christ to be
released through you? Do you want the power
of God to flow through you? Do you want to be
a usable instrument in His hands? Follow the
Savior to the cross. His death and the resurrection that followed bear eternal witness that brokenness brings increased fruitfulness.

Yes, God uses things and people that are broken. In a sense, revival is really nothing more
than the release of God's Spirit flowing through
broken lives. Historical records of revivals bear
this out over and over again, as these few snap-
shots will reveal.

RIVERS OF REVIVAL

During the Welsh Revival in 1904–5, a song
rang out from the contrite hearts and lips of
God's people. "Bend me lower, lower, down at
Jesus' feet," they sang. Through that brokenness, God released a great floodtide of His

Spirit that encompassed the entire principality and overflowed in untold blessing to the world.

Perhaps you have read or heard about the Shantung Revival in China in the late 1920s and early 1930s.[3] Dr. C. L. Culpepper was the director of a large denominational mission in that province. He was part of a group of Christian leaders and missionaries who had been praying for revival.

One night after the prayer meeting, Dr. Culpepper returned to his home and felt pressed to seek the Lord into the late hours of the night. He sensed spiritual need and dryness in his life, but he couldn't put his finger on what the issue might be. He asked, "Lord, what is it in me?"

He listened to the Lord's counsel, and he was shattered by what he heard.

The next morning, he returned to the prayer meeting and confessed to his fellow missionaries and leaders his sin of spiritual pretense and the spiritual impotence that had resulted. He acknowledged that their praise of him as a "good missionary" had caused him to be proud and to steal glory from God. He later said, "My heart was so broken I didn't believe I could live any longer."

Out of Dr. Culpepper's brokenness, God brought brokenness to that entire group of missionaries and national Christian leaders. That, in turn, resulted in a great outpouring of God's Spirit in conviction, confession, and fullness throughout the province. God revived their hearts and countless hearts among those whose lives they touched.

Twenty years later, in another corner of the world, a small band of church leaders prayed earnestly for revival in their community. They were gathered in a small town on the Isle of Lewis, the largest isle of the Outer Hebrides, just off the coast of Scotland. These believers were particularly burdened for the young people of the island who had no interest in spiritual matters and scorned the things of God.

For eighteen months these men met, three nights a week, praying through the night, right on into the early hours of the morning, beseeching God to come and visit in revival. For eighteen months there was no evidence of any change.

Then one night, a young deacon rose to his

feet, opened his Bible, and read from Psalm 24: "Who may ascend into the hill of the Lord? Or

YOUR BROKEN-
NESS MAY BE
THE VERY THING
GOD USES

who may stand in His holy place? He who has clean hands and a pure heart. . . . He shall receive blessing from the Lord" (verses 3–5). Facing the men around him, this young man said, "Brethren, it seems to me to be just so much 'hum-bug' to be waiting and praying as we are, if we ourselves are not rightly related to God."

There in the straw, the men knelt and humbly confessed their own sins to the Lord. Within a short period of time, God had begun to pour out His Spirit in an extraordinary awakening that shook the entire island.

The most dramatic, widespread revival movements in history have begun with a handful of humble-hearted believers whose revived lives and prayers have become sparks that ignited the lives of those around them.

Interestingly, the "most godly" men and women on the scene have generally been the first to humble themselves and have then been used as instruments of revival. Have you been waiting for your mate or children or church leaders to humble themselves so there can be revival in your home or your church? God may be waiting for you to humble yourself; your brokenness may be the very thing He uses to provoke the brokenness of those around you. The greatest hindrance to revival is not others' unwillingness to humble themselves—it is *our* need to humble ourselves and confess our desperate need for His mercy.

Are you seeking to know God in a more intimate way? Do you want the supernatural life of His Spirit to be released through you? Do you long to be able to worship God and to love Him and others with greater freedom? Do you have a desire to be usable in God's hand? Are you conscious of a need for revival in your family, in your church, and in our world? Revival blessings flow to and through those who are truly broken before God. Andrew Murray said it well: "Just as water ever seeks and fills the lowest place, so the moment God finds you abased and empty, His glory and power flow in."

NOTES

1. Jennifer Kennedy Dean, *He Restores My Soul: A Forty-Day Journey Toward Personal Renewal* (Nashville: Broadman & Holman, 1999), 27.

2. Charles H. Spurgeon, *Cheque Book of the Bank of Faith: Daily Readings* (Scotland, Great Britain: Christian Focus Publications, 1996), 210.

3. An account of this revival is recorded in C. L. Culpepper, *Spiritual Awakening: The Shantung Revival* (Atlanta: Home Mission Board, SBC, 1982).

6

JOURNEY
into
BROKENNESS

Being broken is both God's work and ours.
He brings His pressure to bear,
but we have to make the choice. . . .
All day long the choice will be
before us in a thousand ways.

—ROY HESSION[1]

Throughout this book you have been introduced to believers who came to a place of
brokenness before the Lord. What about you?
Have you seen glimpses of your own life in
these pages? Can you honestly say that you
have been truly broken before God?

Perhaps you have experienced genuine brokenness in the past. Are you continuing to walk
in a lifestyle of brokenness today?

You may be saying, "I recognize my need for

a broken and a contrite heart; I want to choose the pathway of brokenness. Where do I begin?"

Brokenness requires both God's initiative and our response. According to the Scripture, there are three primary instruments God uses to bring us to the point of brokenness.

First, *the Word of God* has the power to soften the hardened soil of our hearts and shatter our stubborn self-life. God says, "Is not my word . . . like a hammer that breaks the rock in pieces?" (Jeremiah 23:29). The psalmist stood in awe of the power of His Word: "The voice of the Lord is powerful . . . the voice of the Lord breaks the cedars" (Psalm 29:4–5). Each time we open God's Word, whether in private or public settings, it should be with the intent of allowing the Word to break us. The same Word that serves as a hammer to break us will then become a balm to heal our hearts and a light to guide our footsteps in the pathway of humility.

Second, God uses *circumstances* to expose our need and bring us to the end of ourselves. The circumstance He uses may be a stressful job, a difficult marriage, a chronic illness, a financial crisis, or some other issue that brings pressure to bear on our lives. In the face of such pressure, we can choose to respond in pride, by resisting and resenting the circumstance, or by giving in to despair. Or we can choose to respond in humility, to submit to the hand of God and allow Him to mold and shape us through the pressure.

Third, God has given us *the body of Christ.* As we walk in the light with our fellow believers, they can help us

> WHEN WE STEP INTO THE LIGHT OF GOD'S HOLINESS, OUR LIVES ARE BROUGHT INTO SHARP RELIEF.

see areas where we need to be broken. "Faithful are the wounds of a friend" (Proverbs 27:6)—whether that friend is a pastor, a parent, a partner, or another believer—who loves us enough to point out our spiritual blind spots.

The Word, circumstances, and other believers —these can all be tools to show us our need and create opportunities to choose the pathway of brokenness. The Spirit of God is the arm that wields each of these instruments to bring us to a point of brokenness. However, we must respond to His initiative. How can we cultivate a broken, contrite heart? The following four suggestions will help us enter into a deeper level of personal brokenness:

1. GET A FRESH VISION OF GOD

The closer we get to God, the more clearly we will see ourselves as we really are. As long as we compare ourselves to others, we can always find someone who makes us feel good about how well we are doing. But when we step into the light of God's holiness, our lives are brought into sharp relief. What once may have seemed clean and pure suddenly looks soiled and tarnished. The pure light of His holiness exposes the nooks and crannies, the cracks and crevices of our innermost being.

Throughout the Scripture, when even the holiest men and women were confronted with the awesome holiness of God, they were moved to deep contrition and brokenness before Him.

Take Job, for example. Job was a righteous man; he feared God and lived a blameless life. For reasons known only to God, Job became a bit player in a cosmic drama, acted out between heaven and hell. When he could not fathom God's purposes for the excruciating pain he was forced to endure, and when his so-called friends wrongly assumed that he was being punished for some failure on his part, Job began to reveal a self-righteous heart.

In extended dialogue and debate, Job protested his innocence and begged for the opportunity to defend himself in the courtroom of heaven. Finally, God stepped in—as if He had been patiently waiting for someone to give Him a chance to speak. Through a series of questions that neither Job nor his friends could possibly answer, God revealed Himself in a way that Job had never experienced. God unveiled His greatness, His infinite power, His superior wisdom, His mighty acts, and His unfathomable ways.

When God had finished, Job could hardly breathe. He had been stopped dead in his tracks: "Behold, I am vile; what shall I answer You? I lay my hand over my mouth. . . . I have heard of You by the hearing of the ear, but now my eye sees You. Therefore I abhor myself, and repent in dust and ashes" (Job 40:4; 42:5–6). Job was no longer defensive, no longer claiming innocence or seeing himself as a helpless victim. In the brilliant light of God's majesty, Job was exposed; he now saw himself as a perpetrator and a vile sinner, desperately in need of mercy.

Job had been a good man—his lifestyle was above reproach and his suffering was not directly caused by his sin. Suffering did, however, serve to lift the lid off his heart and expose a deeper level of depravity than he might have otherwise seen. As a result of his encounter with God, Job was not only a good man and a religious man; now he was a broken man.

The prophet Isaiah had a similar experience. In the early chapters of Isaiah, we see this great servant of God pronouncing "woes" on the apostate nation of Israel—"woe" to those who are materialistic; "woe" to those who are relativistic; "woe" to those who are hedonistic; "woe" to those who are sensual and immoral. And he was right. These were terrible blots on the nation, even as they are in our world today.

Then we come to the first verse of Isaiah chapter 6, where Isaiah encounters God in a way he has never seen Him before. The prophet is struck with a vision of the holiness of God—holiness so intense that even the pillars in the temple had the good sense to tremble.

Isaiah no longer sees himself in contrast to all the depraved people around him. Now he sees himself in the light of the holy, high, supreme God of the universe. And what are the first words out of his mouth? No longer is it "Woe to *them.*" Now it is "Woe is *me!*"

After his experience, Isaiah confessed not the sins of the nation but his own sins—"*I am a man of unclean lips.*" In response to his contrite, broken heart, God sent an angel who took a hot coal from the altar of sacrifice. In one searing, painful moment, the hot coal was applied to Isaiah's lips and he was cleansed. Prior to that point, Isaiah had been a good man; he was gifted and committed to God. But in chapter 6, Isaiah came to true brokenness. From then on, he operated not out of natural strength or superiority but out of an intense sense of his own neediness. Isaiah was a broken man.

To know God, to live in His presence, and to be occupied with a vision of His holiness is to know how foolish and frail we are apart from

Him and to be broken from a preoccupation with ourselves.

2. DON'T WAIT FOR GOD TO BREAK YOU— CHOOSE TO BE BROKEN

Jesus identified Himself as the rejected Stone spoken of in the Old Testament: "The stone which the builders rejected has become the chief cornerstone. This was the Lord's doing; it is marvelous in our eyes" (Psalm 118:22–23). He stressed the importance of how we choose to respond to His Lordship: "Whoever falls on that stone will be broken; but on whomever it falls, it will grind him to powder" (Luke 20:18).

Some people who may seem "broken" have not been broken at all. Rather, they have been crushed by their circumstances because of their unwillingness to voluntarily fall on the Rock and be broken. Don't wait for God to break you. "*Humble yourself* under the mighty hand of God" (see 1 Peter 5:6). Fall on the Rock—Christ Jesus, who was broken for you—and cultivate the habit of crying out with the tax collector, "God, be merciful to me a sinner" and with David, "Have mercy on me, O God."

The fact is, we will all be broken—sooner or later. We can choose to be broken or we can wait for God to crush our pride. If we resist the means God provides to lead us to brokenness, we do not avoid brokenness —we simply make it necessary for God to intensify and prolong the process.

We have considered the blessings of brokenness. But we also need to be reminded of the painful price paid by those who refuse to be broken: "He, that being often reproved hardeneth his neck, shall suddenly be destroyed, and that without remedy" (Proverbs 29:1 KJV).

For a time, we may succeed in resisting the will of God; He may allow us to continue walking in the pride of our hearts. But eventually God will bring down everything that exalts itself against Him. There will come a day when every knee will bow and every tongue will confess that Jesus Christ is Lord (see Philippians 2:10–11).

> *The lofty looks of man shall be humbled,*
> *The haughtiness of men shall be bowed down,*
> *And the Lord alone shall be exalted in that day.*
> *For the day of the Lord of hosts*
> *Shall come upon everything proud and lofty,*
> *Upon everything lifted up—*
> *And it shall be brought low.*
> —Isaiah 2:11–12

What is the alternative? Choose the pathway of brokenness. Jennifer Kennedy Dean encourages us to see the difficult circumstances of our lives as "crucifixion moments":

Every time you are confronted with a crucifixion moment, choose to lay down your self-life. Choose to surrender your pride, your expectations, your rights, your demands. Choose the way of the cross. Let someone else get the credit you deserve; forego the opportunity to have the last word; die to the demands of your flesh.[2]

3. ACKNOWLEDGE SPIRITUAL NEED—
TO GOD AND TO OTHERS

If we want to live a lifestyle of humility and brokenness, we must learn to live with the roof off and the walls down. One practical way to do that is to make a habit of acknowledging and verbalizing our spiritual need to God and to others.

Living with the "roof off" toward God is having a heart attitude that says, "It's not my father, not my brother, not my mate, not my kids, not my roommate, not my boss, not the youth director or the pastor—it's *me*, oh Lord, standin' in the need of prayer!" To live with the roof off toward God means that I no longer blame others, but I take personal responsibility for my sin. There is no brokenness where the finger of blame is still pointed at another; brokenness means no excuses, no defending, no rationalizing my sin.

When I acknowledge my need to God, I say,

> Nothing in my hand I bring,
> Simply to Thy cross I cling;

Naked, come to Thee for dress,
Helpless, look to Thee for grace.
Foul, I to the fountain fly;
Wash me, Savior, or I die.[3]

For many of us, it is easier to let the roof off than it is to let the walls down—to be transparent and honest with others. We work so hard at leaving a good impression; we want others to think well of us. But once we have really been contrite and humble before God, it will not be threatening to be humble and honest with others —we have nothing to lose, no reputation to protect—because we have *died*. The broken person is willing to say, "Will you pray for me? I have a need in my life—God is dealing with me in this specific area." Brokenness toward God produces openness toward others. Living with the walls down toward others can become a wonderful means of God's grace in our lives.

When I was in my mid-twenties, God's Spirit began to convict me that I had developed a habit of "exaggerating the truth" in certain situations. ("Exaggeration" is actually a proud, unbroken word for "lying.") Driven to make a good impression on others, I was frequently guilty of "stretching" the truth. Though no one else knew of my deception, and though others might have considered my offenses relatively inconsequential, I experienced an almost suffocating (and blessed!) sense of God's conviction in my heart, and I knew this was something I had to bring into the light.

I agreed with God, confessed my deception, and purposed to begin speaking the truth in every situation. But I soon discovered that lying was a stronghold in my life—it was deeply ingrained. I was hooked and couldn't seem to get set free. Ultimately, the freedom that I needed and longed for began when I was willing to let the walls down. God brought to mind the principle of James 5:16: "Confess your trespasses to one another, and pray for one another, that you may be healed."

I will never forget approaching two godly individuals, acknowledging to them my sin of lying, and asking them to pray for me. It was one of the most difficult things I had ever done, and I would certainly have preferred to work things out alone with the Lord. But the very pride that didn't want to be exposed was the same pride that was causing me to lie. The moment I humbled myself and let down those walls, the pride that had kept me in bondage had its back broken, and I was set free to begin speaking the truth.

Even now, it is not easy for me to put this story in print. But I know that every opportunity to humble myself is an opportunity to get more of His grace, which will enable me to obey God in every area of my life—including being truthful.

4. DO WHATEVER YOU KNOW GOD WANTS YOU TO DO

In most of our lives, there are specific issues about which we know God has revealed something that we have not fully obeyed. Pride causes us to resist or delay our obedience. The humble, broken heart says simply, "Yes, Lord"; "Have Thine own way, Lord. Thou art the Potter; I am the clay."

A number of years ago, I began to realize that the television had become a barrier in my relationship with the Lord. I live alone and had been using the television as a "companion" when I got home after a long day of work. I knew that I would be better off in my walk with the Lord if I turned the TV off—but, for some reason, I resisted yielding to Him. I'm ashamed to admit that I wrestled with this issue for months before I finally surrendered. My resistance had been based on some twisted sense that I would be giving up something I wanted. But the incredible freedom and increased fruitfulness that flowed out of that point of surrender have far surpassed anything that I may have "lost" by giving up my TV viewing.

Some might think, *What's the big deal? Are you trying to tell me I can't watch TV anymore?* I'm not telling you what you can or can't do. Nor am I suggesting that watching television is inherently sinful. I am saying that if we want the blessings of brokenness, we must obey God whenever He begins to deal with our hearts about an issue, regardless of what the issue may be or how hard it may be for our flesh to say yes to God.

For me, the "big deal" was not so much *what* I was watching on television (though when I finally turned it off, I began to realize how desensitized I had become to things that were displeasing to the Lord). The big deal was that I was resisting the direction of the Holy Spirit. The big deal was that I had not considered His authority to be a big deal in my life.

I had not shaken my fist in God's face. However, over a period of time, by ignoring His conviction, I had stiffened my neck and hardened my will against Him. My heart was no longer soft, pliable, and responsive to His leading. The real issue was not whether or not I would watch television. The issue was whether I was going to walk in pride or in brokenness.

You see, though some of us may never blatantly defy God by committing adultery or embezzling money from the church or committing some other egregious sin, all it takes for me—or for you—to get into a position where God is forced to resist us is to refuse to humble ourselves and be broken before Him in one "little" matter. God always resists the proud—whether that proud person is a blasphemer or an adulterer, or a pastor or a homeschooling mom.

"Carl" is a Texas businessman who found himself under the hand of God's conviction a number of years ago. Years earlier, he had been summoned as a witness in a federal court. Under oath, he had purposely given vague answers to direct questions, out of a desire to protect one of the parties involved. He did not tell "the whole truth," as he had sworn to do.

Now, years later, in the middle of the night, God surfaced in his heart this issue that Carl had thought was a "closed case." He knew that if he came clean, he would risk going to prison for perjury. He tried to reason with God; he tried to negotiate a compromise by confessing other sins and offering to surrender other areas of his life. But God wouldn't let him off the hook. Finally, he said, "Yes, Lord." He called the judge's office and explained the situation to an assistant, acknowledging that he had been dishonest on the witness stand and that God had convicted him of the need to make it right. Carl had to wait twelve months before a decision was made that neither side wished to reopen the case.

During that year that seemed to go on forever, God took Carl through a much-needed process of deepening brokenness in his life. When he was first confronted with this issue, by his own testimony, Carl was a proud man. He was a demanding husband and father who was convinced that he was doing fine spiritually and that his wife and children were the ones with

HAS GOD'S
SPIRIT BEEN
TUGGING AT
YOUR HEART?

the real spiritual needs. He admits now that the reason he was concerned about issues in their lives was that he wanted them to make him look good in his community and in his church, where he served as a deacon.

That initial choice to humble himself and call the judge's office proved to be just the first step in an extended process of God stripping away the layers of pride that Carl had been blind to in his life. His obedience in that one difficult issue opened the door for God's grace to be poured into every area of his life. His heart was turned toward his wife and children in a new way and their hearts were turned toward the Lord. He began to experience a deeper level of freedom, compassion, and sensitivity to the Lord and others.

WHAT IS GOD SAYING TO YOU?

As you have been reading, has God's Spirit been tugging at your heart? Is there a step of brokenness He is leading you to take? That step of brokenness may mean:

- Slipping to your knees and acknowledging to God that you *need* Him—that you have been trying to live the Christian life by your own effort, that you have been self-sufficient and tried to live independently of Him.
- Discussing a spiritual need in your life with another believer and asking him or her to pray for you and to help hold you accountable.
- Making a phone call or a visit to humble yourself and seek forgiveness from someone you have sinned against—a parent, a child, a mate, an ex-mate, a friend, a pastor, a neighbor, an employer, or someone else God has laid on your heart. (I had to make one such call today, as I was working on this book.)

- Going before your family, your church family, your discipleship group, or your fellow employees and admitting that you have been a hypocrite and that you have not been living the kind of life you have professed before others.
- Clearing your conscience over something in your past that you have never made right.
- Surrendering your will to God in relation to your future, your career, your marriage, or some other specific issue that He has been speaking to you about.
- Calling off divorce proceedings.
- Selling some possession so you can give more to the Lord's work or help another believer in need.
- Sharing the Gospel with a neighbor or colleague.
- Agreeing to lead a small group or to accept some other responsibility for which you feel inadequate.
- Acknowledging that you have never been truly converted and need to be born again.

You may be thinking, *There's no way I can do that!* Or perhaps you find yourself negotiating with God: "I'll go to anyone, but not that person . . . I'll do anything, but not that one thing . . ."

Dear friend, if you want to experience the blessings of brokenness, if you want to have a revived heart, you must choose to run head-on into whatever it is that your pride is telling you not to do.

As I speak on this message on brokenness in women's conferences all across the country, I generally ask at the close, "How many of you know there is some step of brokenness God wants you to take, but there's a battle going on inside, and your pride is keeping you from taking that step?" Invariably, many hands go up all across the room. I tell them the same thing I want to tell you: The battle inside will stop the moment you wave the white flag of surrender and say "Yes, Lord." The longer you delay, the harder you resist, the more difficult it will be to obey God. Don't hesitate a moment longer. You can't begin to imagine the joy that awaits you on the other side of the Cross, the power of His resurrection life that will be released through your death to self, and the wholeness that will emerge out of your brokenness.

Oh Father, we confess our great need of Your grace—grace to let You search our hearts; grace to offer to You the sacrifice of a broken, contrite heart; grace to put to death our pride and self-will; grace to walk in the pathway of humility, as our beloved Savior humbled Himself for us; and grace to keep looking to Him as our only hope of eternal salvation. Through our broken-ness, may Christ be seen, magnified, loved, and worshiped by others, till He returns to make all things new. Amen.

NOTES

1. Roy Hession, *The Calvary Road* (Fort Washington, Pa.: Christian Literature Crusade, 1990), 23, 25.
2. Jennifer Kennedy Dean, *He Restores My Soul: A Forty-Day Journey Toward Personal Renewal* (Nashville: Broadman & Holman, 1999), 33.
3. "Rock of Ages" by Augustus M. Toplady.

AFTERWORD:
*A Personal
Testimony*

*For, as to have a broken heart,
is to have an excellent thing,
so to keep this broken heart tender,
is also very advantageous.*

—JOHN BUNYAN[1]

In a sense, I wish I had waited another twenty years or so before agreeing to write this book. As I have written, I have been faced with the reality that my life is still wading around in the shallows of a vast, deep subject. It seems that I have only touched the hem of the garment of His ways, when it comes to understanding and experiencing what it means to have a "broken and contrite spirit." But I do know that such a heart is something that God treasures and seeks and empowers. And, in spite of frequent failures, I have embarked on a daily, lifelong pilgrimage to cultivate the kind of heart He revives.

I have described the gathering in July 1995 when God moved in such a gracious way to bring men and women to a point of brokenness before Him. During that week, hundreds of men and women were revived as they offered to God the sacrifice of a broken and contrite heart.

As is generally the case when we minister to others, God's purpose that week was not just to change those who heard me speak. He knew there was a need for a deeper level of humility and brokenness in my own life.

That occasion resulted in some significant changes and challenges in my life and ministry. In the weeks and months that followed, tens of thousands of audio- and videotapes of the message on brokenness were distributed throughout the nation and around the world. As word spread of what had happened, I was presented with many new ministry opportunities, including a dramatic increase in invitations to speak at other gatherings.

Many people who had heard the message, either in Colorado or on tape, wrote to tell their stories. Others stopped me along the way to share how God had used the message in their lives or in their church family. I was truly grateful and deeply awed by what God had done. But all the publicity poured fresh fuel on a fire I had battled most of my life—a craving for human applause and recognition, or what the Bible calls "love of the praise of men."

Long before 1995 I had repented of this sin, and out of that brokenness had experienced a great measure of freedom and victory. But in the months following the Campus Crusade conference, I gradually found myself once again in bondage to this lust for human praise. I would find myself relishing hearing people talking about how God had used me. I was quick to pass along to others complimentary letters, e-mails, and write-ups about my ministry with the motive of having them think highly of me. I loved seeing my name in print, and at times would take steps to ensure that full credit was given. Even as I write this, I am grieved by the tendency of my heart to embezzle the glory that rightly belongs only to Him.

As the scope of my ministry grew exponentially, so did the battle with pride and self-exaltation—even as I was traveling around the country delivering what had become a "signature message" on humility and brokenness. As is always the case with sin and pride, the answer is to get out "into the light"—to let the roof off and the walls down. I had stepped into the light with God, but I realized I needed to humble myself before others in order to put the ax to the root of this poisonous pride in my heart.

One morning I sensed the Lord directing me to write a letter to about a dozen of my "praying friends"—men and women whom I knew cared for my soul. I admitted this matter to them and asked them to pray that I would be delivered. The simple act of writing and sending that letter was an important step of brokenness for me and began a process of personal revival and restoration. That initial step of humility became a means by which God brought much-needed grace into my life.

One of those individuals wrote and gave an idea that had come to him as he had prayed for me:

Perhaps for a season you might collect letters of commendation, praise, and anything that could be the occasion for pride. Do you have a fireplace? If so, once a week, light the fire, and then read through at least a few of them. Then tell the Lord that you know everything will someday be tried by fire and only the gold, silver, and truly precious things will last.

At that point, toss some or all of the letters into the fireplace as a symbolic gesture. You might pray (in your words): "Lord, I put the fire to all of these words that could be a cause to puff me up or create pride. You alone know what is pure before You and what is truly lasting. I want only that which truly pleases You to flow out of my life!" Somehow I sense that this gesture of denial or submission would deeply impact your heart.

As I read this suggestion, I had an unmistakable sense that God had spoken through His servant. My mind went immediately to a particular bulging file in my study that contained "memorabilia" related to that week in the summer of 1995. In that file, I had placed many flattering letters, published accounts and articles about the event, reprints of my message in other publications, requests for permission to reproduce, and other complimentary responses.

God showed me that the contents of that file had served to fuel my pride and had been a means of the Enemy gaining a foothold in my life. I don't think I had opened that file in the two years that had passed, except to add items to it. But its very existence had been meaningful to me. It was symbolic of the enhanced reputation I had experienced and relished in the wake of that divine visitation. I had always known I could go back at some low point and be affirmed by the praise contained within that manila folder.

As the Lord would have it, a couple of weeks after receiving his letter I was scheduled to be in the city where this man and his wife live (never having been there before). I contacted them, explained how the Lord had spoken to me, and asked if they would be willing to meet with me when I was in town to witness the burning of this material. They graciously agreed.

A journal entry I made at that time gives a personal glimpse into what was going on in my heart:

There is a dying involved in walking through this process—dying to being able to ever go back and reread the words of praise, dying to anyone else ever reading and being impressed by what's in there, dying to ever being able to draw affirmation or a sense of personal worth from those flattering words.

This exercise gets to the heart of some of the deepest needs in my life. Flesh dies hard—but I know that beyond the brokenness, there will be wholeness; beyond the death, there will be a new experience of His abundant life.

Grant, oh God, I pray, a deeper level of brokenness, repentance, and humility than I have previously known. Put the ax to the root of the pride in my life. I do repent of that hideous, self-congratulating, self-exalting, self-seeking pride that has so deeply tainted my motives, my thoughts, and my service for You. Please break the bondage of pride in my life. Set me free to love, exalt, and worship You, and You alone.

More than anything, I want You to be glorified in my life.

A couple of weeks later, that couple and I met together in their living room, seated in front of the fireplace. Following a time of Scripture reading and prayer, I placed all the contents of that file—one handful at a time—into the fire, having already offered it all up to the Lord in my heart.

In the days that followed, God began to grant an unusually sweet sense of His presence, I found my heart growing in tenderness for Him, and His Word was quickened to my heart in richer and more personal ways than had been true in a long time. Shortly after that particular breaking process, God began to provide fresh insight and direction in relation to future ministry.

You may or may not particularly relate to my battle with craving recognition and praise. The pride in your heart may manifest itself in ways that are quite different. Regardless of the specific nature of the battleground, the point is that pride and self must die. Then, through our broken-

ness, we will experience the release of the res-
urrection life and the sweet fragrance of the
Lord Jesus and the free-flowing power of His
Holy Spirit.

NOTE

1. John Bunyan, *Acceptable Sacrifice; or the Excellency of a Broken Heart,* vol. 1(Edinburgh: Banner of Truth Trust, 1999), 712.

Dear friend,

I need revival. My heart is so "prone to wander, . . . prone to leave the God I love." And we need revival in the church—a supernatural work of the Spirit breathing new life into our walk with God and our witness in the world. As we have seen, a broken and a contrite heart is a prerequisite to revival, whether personal or corporate.

As we continue in the pursuit of God and the pathway of revival, we discover another indispensable heart attitude: *wholehearted surrender to Jesus as Lord.* Our natural instincts resist the idea of wholly surrendering ourselves to the will and control of another. However, the truth is that we will never be fully free until we relinquish control and wave the white flag of surrender to our sovereign Lord.

In *Surrender*, the next book in the *Revive Our Hearts* series, we will explore what it means to live a life of surrender, sacrifice, and slavery to the Lord Jesus, and how such a life is the only path to true freedom and joy.

I invite you to join me in pressing on to know Him, so that our lives might bring Him pleasure and that others might be drawn to bow the knee before our glorious, matchless King.

Warmly,

Nancy

Nancy Leigh DeMoss has produced numerous booklets, audiotapes, and videotapes to promote personal and corporate revival. Her primary focus is helping women experience freedom, fullness, and fruitfulness through Christ. For a catalogue of available resources, or to learn more about the ministry of *Revive Our Hearts* radio or conferences, contact:

Life Action Ministries
P.O. Box 31
Buchanan, MI 49107

(269) 684-5905
E-mail: Info@LifeAction.org
www.ReviveOurHearts.com